You've Always Been There for Me

For a list of all the titles in the series, please see the last page of the book.

You've Always Been There for Me

~

*Understanding the Lives of
Grandchildren Raised by
Grandparents*

RACHEL E. DUNIFON

R

Rutgers University Press
New Brunswick, Camden, and Newark, New Jersey, and London

Library of Congress Cataloging-in-Publication Data

Names: Dunifon, Rachel E. (Rachel Elizabeth), author.
Title: You've always been there for me : understanding the lives of
grandchildren raised by grandparents / Rachel Dunifon.
Description: New Brunswick : Rutgers University Press, 2018. |
Series: The Rutgers series in childhood studies | Includes
bibliographical references and index.
Identifiers: LCCN 2017056009 | ISBN 9780813584003 (cloth : alk. paper) |
ISBN 9780813583990 (pbk. : alk. paper)
Subjects: LCSH: Grandparents as parents—United States. |
Grandchildren—United States. | Grandparent and child—United States. |
Families—United States.
Classification: LCC HQ759.9 .D854 2018 | DDC 306.874/50973—dc23 LC
record available at https://lccn.loc.gov/2017056009

A British Cataloging-in-Publication record for this book is available from the
British Library.

∞ The paper used in this publication meets the requirements of the
American National Standard for Information Sciences—Permanence of
Paper for Printed Library Materials, ANSI Z39.48-1992.

www.rutgersuniversitypress.org

Manufactured in the United States of America

For John, Jimmy, and Will, who show me each
day the meaning of love and family

Contents

You've Always Been There for Me

Introduction

Lindsey, age sixteen, came to live with her great-grandmother, Lucille, when she was three years old. Lindsey's mother, Angie, gave birth to Lindsey as a teenager; Lindsey's father was murdered shortly after she was born. After Lindsey was born, Angie increasingly asked Lucille to watch Lindsey while she went out with her friends. Finally, fed up with the repeated and unpredictable requests to watch the baby, Lucille gave Angie an ultimatum: hand over temporary custody of Lindsey or Lucille would no longer watch her. Angie agreed and has never asked to resume custody of Lindsey. She lives just over an hour away and sees Lindsey regularly. In fact, Lindsey sometimes spends school breaks with Angie. However, Lindsey is acutely aware that Angie's role in her life is not that of a typical mother. As Lindsey goes through her teenage years, she expresses increasing awareness of, and sadness about, her living situation, noting that she used to call Lucille "Mom" but no longer does so. She says, "When you think of family, you think of Mom, Dad, two kids, and a dog. . . . And then, when you're raised by a grandparent, you're thinking 'this isn't my mom. I ain't got no dad.' Everything is so off, and that's always going to be inside of me. Reality. Face it. This isn't my mom." Raised by grandparents herself, Lucille, now age seventy-four, sees the pain that Lindsey is going through and sympathizes, saying, "I wanted my mom, and I know the feeling."

Lindsey and Lucille are not alone. Currently, 1.6 million children in the United States are being raised by their grandparents with no parents living in the household,[1] in what I refer to in this book as "grandfamilies." A variety of reasons lead children to come live with their grandparents, and this living arrangement can be found among families from all walks of life. Even President Barack Obama spent some of his childhood raised by his maternal grandparents.[2] By providing care to children whose parents are not able to care for them and keeping children connected to their families, grandparents play an important role in today's society. One study estimates that, by providing care to children whose parents are not able to raise them, grandparents save the government $6.5 billion per year.[3]

Despite this, and as this book shows, grandfamilies often exist under the radar, hidden from social service agencies, policymakers, and the general public. Researchers, too, have not given grandfamilies the attention they deserve. This certainly was the case for me. During graduate school and in the early stages of my career as a faculty member, my research agenda focused on children's living arrangements, examining how living in single-parent and cohabiting-parent households influences the development of children. When I started my faculty position at Cornell University, I began connecting with policymakers and practitioners who work with families, keen to share with them the results of my research. I eagerly presented to them the latest information on children growing up with single mothers or those living with cohabiting parents, and the policymakers and practitioners politely listened. However, time after time, I was asked questions about one group of children that I could not answer: What about children who are being raised by their grandparents? What do we know about them, and how can we better address their needs? Policymakers observed that an increasing proportion of their welfare caseload was made up of such families. Practitioners working with families struggled to incorporate grandparents raising grandchildren into their traditional parent education classes. They looked to me to shed light on grandfamilies from a research perspective, and I was humbled to realize that, despite my training in family research, I had nothing to tell them.

This gap in my knowledge led me to examine the research literature on grandfamilies. I found that, while some excellent research examines grandfamily lives, few studies shed light on what truly interests me and is essential for those working with grandfamilies: What is life really like "under the roof" of grandfamily households? What do we know about the complex relationships and circumstances of families like Lindsey and Lucille's? How do such families come about and what role do the absent parents play in the lives of children living in grandfamilies? What challenges do grandparents raising their grandchildren face, especially during the teenage years, and what unique strengths and advantages exist in such families? Finally, what policies and programs might best address these families' unique circumstances and needs? Only by addressing these questions can effective policies and programs emerge to address grandfamily needs.

I noticed that a key piece lacking in previous research on grandfamilies was the voices of the grandchildren themselves. Much research on grandfamily households consists of interviews of the grandparents only, who are asked to report on the well-being and characteristics of all members of the household, including their grandchildren. While important, this provides a limited perspective that is shaded by the grandparents' experiences. In order to address the questions that interest me, what family dynamics are really like in grandfamilies, I knew I was going to need to talk to both grandchildren and grandparents. Finally, given my interest in getting "under the roof" of grandfamily households, I knew I needed to go beyond traditional paper and pencil survey–based methods of data collection. I wanted to understand how grandparents and grandchildren interact with each other when discussing issues central to family life, what their relationship is like, and how they understand their unique family situation. To do that, I needed a multimethod approach, including video data of grandparent–grandchild conversations that would allow me to observe and understand communication, relationship quality, and interpersonal interactions in grandfamily households.

To fill these gaps in the research and to increase our knowledge of grandfamily households, I embarked on an ambitious data-collection project, funded by the William T. Grant Foundation Scholars Program. I gathered a wide range of data from grandparents and teenaged grandchildren in grandfamilies across the state of New York, using a multimethod approach that included surveys, videotaped observations, and open-ended interviews. I went out of my way to obtain a sample as diverse as possible and worked with community agencies to recruit families as well as to develop the questions that these families would be asked.

This book is based on those data, using the stories of the families who graciously shared their experiences with me to shed light on life "under the roof" of grandfamily households. In doing so, I uncover several important aspects of family life in such households.

First, I learned that the circumstances by which children came to live with their grandparents are complex but typically involve parents voluntarily choosing to give up their children, rather than someone else forcing them to do so.

Oftentimes, such decisions are wrapped up in parents' mental health and substance abuse issues.

In addition, despite not living in the household, parents often still play a key role in the lives of those living in grandfamilies. This, particularly when combined with parents' mental health and substance abuse issues, can present challenges to children and grandparents alike, as parents can come in and out of the lives of their children, may not reinforce good behavior (and could even encourage children to engage in inappropriate behaviors), and may create confusion regarding their roles in the lives of their children.

Most children in my study came to live with their grandparents very early in childhood, and all parties involved expected them to remain there until moving out on their own. Despite this longevity, though, I found that children's understanding of how they came to live with their grandparents and what role their parent plays in their life is complex and changing and can affect the grandparent–grandchild relationship. As the grandchildren grow older, and especially during adolescence, they begin to question their living situation, asking who their "real" parents are and how they should relate to their parents and grandparents. This questioning and its impact on the grandparent–grandchild relationship can be particularly challenging during adolescence.

I also learned that grandfamily households face several challenges, a key one being the health concerns of both the grandparent and the grandchild. Grandparents struggled with keeping up with young grandchildren while facing the health-related challenges of older age. Grandchildren themselves had strikingly high levels of health issues, particularly attention-deficit disorder and other socioemotional problems. Other challenges include raising grandchildren on limited financial resources, particularly for grandparents not working and not married. Grandparents also face the challenges of parenting for a second time, older and wiser, but across a wide generation gap and in a very different societal context than they faced the first time around.

Finally, and most importantly, a key finding of my study was that grandparents and grandchildren exhibit a great deal of warmth and appreciation for the unique roles they are able to play in each other's lives. My research team and I were taken aback by the repeated, genuine, and endearing expressions of love and warmth that the grandchildren we interviewed—teenagers all—communicated to and about their grandparents. Grandparents, too, repeatedly told us how grateful they were to have the chance to raise and develop a very special relationship with their grandchildren, detailing their appreciation for the numerous benefits they got out of raising them. Despite the financial, health, emotional, and other challenges faced by grandfamilies, love and warmth were very much a dominant theme in our conversations with grandparents and grandchildren.

As mentioned earlier, this book focuses on teenagers living in grandfamilies, and there are several reasons that I decided to focus on this particular age group. Adolescence is an exciting time of identity formation and development, a time when children face the key tasks of discovering who they are, particularly in relation to family and others.[4] This can present challenges for any teenager, but especially for those raised by their grandparents, who reside in a unique and oftentimes fluid living arrangement with what is often a lack of clarity about the roles that their parents and grandparents play in their lives. Such youths may feel different and isolated from their peers, becoming increasingly aware of how their living arrangement differs from that of their friends. As indicated by Lindsey's interview at the start of this chapter, teenagers in grandfamilies may begin to question who their "real" parents are, leading to complicated dynamics between them, their grandparents, and their parents. In this way, increased awareness of and ambiguity about family roles can cause youths living in grandfamilies to reevaluate their family lives and positions in them.

Adolescence is not only difficult for youths in grandfamilies. Grandparents can find the teenage years challenging as well. Anyone raising a teenager understands the joy of watching a child begin to discover his own sense of self as well as the difficulties posed by the combination of an increased desire for autonomy along with changing hormones and complicated peer interactions. For grandparents raising their grandchildren, these difficulties are often heightened by unique factors, including a larger gap between generations, changes in child-rearing norms compared to when they were raising their children, the difficulties of raising a teenager on a fixed retirement income, and the limited energy they may have due to health or other concerns.

A final reason that I chose to interview teenagers in grandfamilies is because I wanted to hear their stories in their own words. Adolescence may be a challenging time, but as will become clear in this book, teenagers are remarkably honest and insightful when telling their stories. I was impressed and honored by the way that the teenagers I interviewed opened up in discussing even very sensitive and challenging issues. Each time I read through or listen to what they said, I laugh at their sense of humor, cringe at their brutal honesty, and lament the very difficult situations many of them have been through. I will always remember the girl who, when asked to name a topic that she and her grandmother disagree about, immediately answered, "Dragons!" Nor will I forget the boy who, while still on camera, whispered to his appalled grandmother that they should just take the money that they were to be paid at the end of the interview now and run—nor the boy who asked if he could get his payment in one-dollar bills, so he could "fan it out."

I remain grateful for the chance to get to know these unique teens and their grandparents. I hope that this book makes their voices and stories come alive and can ultimately increase our appreciation for them and inform the development of programs designed to heighten their numerous strengths and address the unique challenges grandfamilies face.

Grandfamilies in the United States

Before describing the grandfamilies featured in this book, it is useful to see a statistical portrait of such households in the United States as a whole. Such information is available from the U.S. Census Bureau and is presented in table I.1, where the characteristics of U.S. children in grandfamilies are compared to the average U.S. child. As the census data show, children in grandfamilies are more likely to be African American than are children in the general U.S. population; 29 percent of children in grandfamilies are African American, compared to 14 percent in the United States as a whole. The prevalence of Hispanic children is similar across children in grandfamilies and other U.S. children, while the percentage of Asian children is lower in grandfamilies (2 percent versus 5 percent in the United States as a whole). Children in grandfamilies are also more likely to be poor or near-poor than the average U.S. child; two-thirds live at or near the federal poverty line, meaning that a family of four lives on a total household income of $46,000 per year or less. Not surprising given this higher economic need, rates of public assistance such as food assistance, public health insurance, cash assistance, and free or reduced-price lunch are higher among grandfamily grandchildren than other children in the United States.

TABLE I.1. Characteristics of children in grandfamilies

	GRANDFAMILY CHILDREN	U.S. CHILDREN
Age		
Mean	8.44 (5.2)	8.61 (5.1)
< 6	0.34	0.32
6–11	0.33	0.34
12–17	0.33	0.34
Race/ethnicity		
Black	0.29	0.14
White	0.39	0.52
Asian	0.02	0.05
Hispanic	0.23	0.24
Other	0.07	0.06
Male	0.52	0.51
U.S. born	0.97	0.96
English primary language	0.91	0.84
Income-to-needs ratio		
Mean	1.88 (1.4)	2.56 (1.6)
< 100%	0.33	0.22
1–200%	0.30	0.22
2–300%	0.16	0.17
300–400%	0.09	0.12
400%+	0.12	0.27
Food stamps / Supplemental Nutrition Assistance Program	0.42	0.26
Health insurance		
Private	0.26	0.59
Public	0.71	0.39
Cash assistance receipt	0.20	0.04
School lunch receipt	0.60	0.45
Live in public housing	0.09	0.07
Grandparent type		
Just grandmother	0.45	
Just grandfather	0.07	
Both	0.48	
Lives with a sibling	0.37	0.78

(continued)

TABLE I.1. Characteristics of children in grandfamilies
(*continued*)

	GRANDFAMILY CHILDREN	U.S. CHILDREN
Lives with aunt/uncle	0.30	0.05
Lives with other relative	0.47	0.06
Number of people in household	4.66 (2.1)	4.53 (1.6)
Under 18	2.31 (1.5)	2.45 (1.3)
Over 18	2.53 (1.4)	2.16 (0.9)
N	1,626,763	73,281,085

SOURCE: Natasha Pilkauskas and Rachel Dunifon, "Children Living with Grandparents: Prevalence, Characteristics, and Complexity," unpublished manuscript, 2016.

NOTE: Standard deviations in parentheses. All statistics are weighted to provide population estimates.

Looking at living arrangements, the census data presented in table I.1 tells us that the vast majority of children in grandfamily households live with a grandmother, and very few involve situations in which a single grandfather is raising his grandchildren. For example, in the United States, 48 percent of grandchildren in grandfamilies live with two grandparents, while 45 percent live with just their grandmothers. Table I.1 also indicates that children in grandfamilies are much less likely to live with a sibling than children in the United States as a whole, with only 37 percent having a sibling living in the household, compared to 78 percent of children in the United States on average. This suggests that it is common for children in grandfamilies to have a sibling living outside of their household. Finally, the data presented in table I.1 show that grandfamily households are much more complex than the average U.S. household: almost one-third contain the child's aunt or uncle, and almost half contain other relatives, such as cousins. Because of this, grandfamily households are larger than the average U.S. household, containing fewer children but more adults than the average.

Table I.2 presents information on the characteristics of grandparents in grandfamilies, comparing them to the average U.S. parent. Grandparents heading grandfamilies are less likely to be married (51 percent) than the average U.S. parent (69 percent). Grandparents are much less likely to be employed than heads of other U.S. households with children, with only 53 percent employed, compared to 80 percent of U.S. parents; and they have lower levels of education compared to heads of other U.S. households with children, with only 12 percent having graduated from college, compared to 35 percent of parents in the United States. Rates of disability among grandparents in grandfamily households are strikingly high, with 20 percent reporting that they receive supplemental security disability benefits, compared to only 4 percent among the average U.S. parent.

Looking at trends over the past twenty-five years, data show that the prevalence of grandfamilies increased slightly during the 1990s and has since remained relatively steady at just over 2 percent of all U.S. children, representing about 1.6 million children in any given year. Other work that I have done with my colleagues Mariana Amorim and Natasha Pilkauskas shows that from birth to age eighteen, 5 percent of all U.S. children will ever live in a grandfamily. That number differs greatly by race, standing at 3.5 percent for white children, 5 percent for Hispanic children, 1.7 percent for Asian children, and 10 percent for black children.[5]

Beyond the results of the study presented in this book, other information shedding light on grandfamilies comes from a unique dataset called the Fragile Families and Child Well-Being Survey,[6] a study of relatively disadvantaged children born in large U.S. cities between 1998 and 2000. The Fragile Families study is one of the very few surveys that interviews children who are not living with their parents and contains a large enough sample of children being raised

TABLE I.2. Characteristics of grandparents and parents

	GRANDFAMILY GRANDPARENTS	U.S. PARENTS
Age		
Mean	56.55 (10.6)	40.17 (9.4)
Race/ethnicity		
Black	0.27	0.13
White	0.48	0.60
Asian	0.02	0.06
Hispanic	0.20	0.20
Other	0.03	0.02
Male	0.35	0.47
U.S. born	0.84	0.79
English primary language	0.79	0.74
Relationship		
Married	0.51	0.69
Separated/divorced	0.26	0.15
Widowed	0.11	0.01
Never married	0.11	0.15
Education		
Less than high school	0.23	0.10
High school	0.41	0.29
Some college	0.24	0.26
College or greater	0.12	0.35
Labor-force participation		
Employed	0.53	0.80
Unemployed	0.03	0.04
Not in labor force	0.44	0.15
Supplemental Security Income receipt	0.20	0.04
Health insurance		
Private	0.54	0.71
Public	0.48	0.19
N	1,038,519	33,055,632

SOURCE: Natasha Pilkauskas and Rachel Dunifon, "Children Living with Grandparents: Prevalence, Characteristics, and Complexity," unpublished manuscript, 2016.

NOTE: Standard deviations in parentheses. All statistics are weighted to provide population estimates. The grandparent or parent is the reference person; in cases where they were not the reference person, one parent/grandparent was randomly selected to be included.

by grandparents to be able to examine this group. It is the only survey that includes not only information about grandparents and the grandchildren they are raising but also information about the parents who are no longer living with their own children. I will discuss that information in a later chapter. My colleague Natasha Pilkauskas and I have examined the subsample of eighty-four children in the Fragile Families study who live in grandfamilies and were able to glean some more detailed information about such families than what is found in census data.[7] From our analysis, we know that 75 percent of Fragile Families children in grandfamilies live with their maternal, rather than paternal, grandparents. We also learned that the children had been living with their grandparents for the majority of their lives (they were aged nine at the time of our data analysis), and 85 percent of the grandparents interviewed in that study expected to raise their grandchildren until at least age eighteen.

Therefore, the research that has occurred to date provides us with some good information about the characteristics of grandparents and grandchildren in grandfamilies, focusing on aspects such as race and ethnicity, poverty, and education. Such statistics, while informative, do not address the key question central to this book: what is life like in grandfamily households? To gather that information, I had to embark on my own study.

Family Life in Grandfamily Households

First, though, I needed to ground myself in existing research and theories on family life in general and grandfamilies in particular. Researchers draw on a variety of theories to inform their studies of family life, and these frameworks are useful when thinking about grandfamilies. For example, life-course theory[8] and family systems theory[9] emphasize that families are more than just collections of individuals but are instead complex systems with unique characteristics and patterns. Individuals in families have interdependent and nuanced reciprocal relationships with each other that unfold over time.[10] When thinking about grandfamilies, this means that the actions of one family member (the parent) cause another member (the grandparent) to take on the responsibility of raising a third (the grandchild). In addition, the parent can continue to play a central role in the dynamics of the grandfamily even when living outside of the household. Based on the perspectives of the life-course and family systems theories, and in order to best capture the complex and interconnected lives of family members, my study involves interviews with both grandparents and grandchildren in grandfamilies, understanding that it is not possible to understand one without the other. In addition, by focusing on the role of the absent parent in grandfamily households, I am able to examine the complex ways in which family members are intertwined, even when not living together.

Another relevant perspective often used by researchers studying family dynamics is role theory, which emphasizes how individuals' behavior differs depending on the role that they play in a given situation.[11] For example, my behavior and others' expectations about my behavior are different when I am at home, in the role of mother and wife, from my behavior at work, in the role of professor. When roles and expected behaviors are clear and obvious, things generally operate smoothly, as people have a good understanding of how they and others are expected to behave in certain situations. I understand that my children have different expectations of me than do my colleagues, and I am able to behave accordingly, based on that knowledge.

Difficulties can emerge, however, when someone is not clear about the role she should play in a certain situation or in relation to others—or when she is expected to play two conflicting roles at the same time.[12] For grandparents raising grandchildren, confusion often exists about whether they should take on the role of parents, enforcing rules and discipline, or whether they should behave more like traditional grandparents, focusing on fun and spoiling the grandchildren. Both the parent and grandparent might each think that she herself should play the parental role, or each of them may assume that the other one will do so, leading to confusion and conflict. Other times, the grandparent might know that she should act like a parent, providing guidance and discipline, but wishes she could instead behave like a "typical" grandparent by spoiling the child. In yet other situations, the grandparent may be clear about taking on a parental role, but the grandchild might not accept it, refusing to abide by the rules and rejecting the grandparent's role as rule-enforcer. Confusion about roles within grandfamilies can affect both grandparents and grandchildren in negative ways.[13] In order to better understand this, and informed by role theory, a key goal of this study is to investigate the ways in which both grandparents and grandchildren see their roles in grandfamilies, as well as how they perceive the role of the absent parent.

This book joins a large body of research examining the complex situations in which today's U.S. children reside.[14] Dramatic changes in family life occurring in recent decades include increases in births outside of marriage, cohabitation, and divorce. Recent decades have also seen an increased tendency for parents to have children with more than one partner, oftentimes called "multipartnered fertility," meaning that parents have children living in more than one household, creating complicated circumstances in which mothers and fathers may find it difficult to devote time and financial resources to their children.[15] As a result, U.S. children today live in much more complicated circumstances than in previous decades. Less than half (46 percent) of U.S. children live in what we typically consider a "nuclear family," with two married parents in their first marriage; in 1960, 73 percent of children lived in such a family, and in 1980, 61 percent did so. Today, 41 percent of U.S. children are born outside of marriage; other children are born to married parents but later experience divorce, with 6 percent of U.S. children currently living with a stepparent.[16] As a result, it is not uncommon for partners, children, and spouses to move in and out of children's increasingly complex households. Less-advantaged and racial and ethnic minority children are more likely to live in complex households (those without both biological parents). For example, today, over 70 percent of black children and 50 percent Hispanic children are born to unmarried mothers.[17]

Many studies examine the implications of these dramatic changes for families and children and, in general, find that families in which children are not living with both biological married parents face financial challenges, difficulties in effective parenting, and poorer outcomes for children. Given that children from less-advantaged backgrounds, such as those with younger and less well-educated mothers, are more likely to live in complex households, this raises concerns about increasing and entrenched patterns of inequality, in which some children face numerous disadvantages that can impact their well-being over the long run.[18] This line of family research, which is very large and robust, includes a variety of studies, ranging from examinations of large-scale longitudinal survey data to rich ethnographic accounts. However, this research focuses on situations in which a child lives with at least one biological parent. Oftentimes missing is a broader examination of the complex living situations in which today's children reside, specifically a consideration of the lives of children who live with neither parent. Against the backdrop of dramatic changes in American family life, it is important to broaden our understanding of family complexity to consider the functioning of a wider set of families, including those in which children are raised by their grandparents.

Speaking to this need, a growing body of research has begun to make important contributions to our understanding of grandfamilies. Here I briefly review what we know from these previous studies and highlight what is not yet known. Research tells us that a variety of often overlapping reasons lead children to live with their grandparents, including substance abuse, child abuse and neglect, incarceration, mental health issues, young age, or death.[19] We also know from previous studies, and this book confirms, that the vast majority of children being raised by their grandparents enter this living arrangement as a result of a voluntary arrangement between the parent and grandparent, as opposed to through a situation in which the child welfare system removed the child from the parental home due to abuse and neglect. It is very rare for grandchildren (fewer than 10 percent) to enter grandfamilies under state custody as part of the foster care system.[20]

Research that has been conducted to date tells us that grandfamilies face numerous challenges, including grandparental health problems, stress, and financial strain. As described earlier, grandparents may struggle with role conflict, wishing they could behave as grandparents but needing to fill the role of parent. Grandparents also face financial difficulties that come with raising a child on what is often a fixed income, including housing issues when taking in an unexpected child and the need to readjust their financial plans for the later years of their lives. These challenges can result in feelings of stress, depression, and isolation.[21]

Perhaps not surprisingly, given the traumatic experiences they have been through, grandfamily children often have elevated behavior problems and poorer academic outcomes compared to other children in the United States,[22] as well as high levels of health problems. Research tells us that grandparents in grandfamilies have uniquely high levels of health problems as well, even compared to other grandparents who are not raising their grandchildren.[23]

Family scholars are also beginning to understand the nature of the involvement of nonresident parents in grandfamilies. Studies highlight the fact that contact with nonresident parents (especially mothers) remains high in grandfamilies,[24] despite their absence from the household. Grandparents often play a key role in brokering the relationship between nonresident parents and grandchildren, encouraging parental contact and providing the parent with access to the grandchild.[25] However, this contact is made complicated by the fact that grandparents often exhibit strong feelings of anger and loss toward their own children, expressing deep disappointment that their children, whom they raised and whom they still love, have made choices or are in situations in which they cannot or will not raise their own children.[26] While parental involvement in grandfamilies is frequent, the nature of the contact between nonresident parents and grandchildren can be stressful. Few studies, however, have interviewed children directly about the role of their parents in their lives. The few that have suggest that children being raised by a grandparent often report feelings of anger, distrust, or loss when discussing their absent mothers.[27] Others do not exhibit such negative feelings but see their mothers more as friends than parents. No previous study has gathered video data capturing the emotions and conversations of both grandparents and grandchildren as they discuss this topic. This book does so.

Researchers are also beginning to understand the parenting behaviors of grandparents in grandfamilies, with evidence suggesting that grandparents have some concerns, particularly around the challenges of parenting teens. While these concerns are real, grandparents also report that, in many ways, they are better parents "the second time around," with greater wisdom, maturity, and senses of what is really important when it comes to raising children.[28] Raising grandchildren can also infuse grandparents with a sense of purpose in their later years.[29] Indeed, research shows that compared to nonrelative foster parents, grandparents exhibit better parenting skills, perhaps suggesting the benefits of the increased wisdom, experience, and maturity that they bring to the role.[30] Studies also highlight a great deal of warmth and gratitude between grandparents and grandchildren in grandfamilies.[31] At the same time, challenges exist in the grandparent–grandchild relationship, including a generation gap leading to rules that the grandchild perceives as unfair and when age or health problems combine to make it difficult to keep up with active grandchildren.[32]

Despite the important insights offered by this previous research, some key gaps remain. First, few studies contain interviews with the grandchildren themselves. Instead, most relied on grandparents to report on the well-being of the entire family. In order to truly understand the dynamics within grandfamily households, we need to hear from the grandchildren themselves. In addition, other studies relied on surveys or separate interviews of grandparents and grandchildren but did not collect video data of grandparents and grandchildren actually interacting with each other. My study does collect such data, allowing me to see grandparents and grandchildren talking together about both enjoyable and difficult aspects of family life. This approach allows me to "get under the roof" of grandfamily households in order to truly understand the nature of the interactions between grandparents and grandchildren and allows me to contribute to the existing body of research on this important topic.

About the Study

This book is based on interviews with fifty-nine families in which grandparents were raising their grandchildren with none of the children's parents living in the household. The interviews occurred between February and August of 2009 and took place throughout New York State. In order to recruit families, I worked with the very people who generated my interest in this topic in the first place—those working at community agencies providing services to grandfamilies. Such services ranged from support groups, to resource guides, to parenting classes and programs for youths. Many, but not all, of these community agencies were part of the Cornell Cooperative Extension system. I talked to community educators from these agencies, described my goals, and asked them to help me think through topics to cover in the study as well as the best way to gather data from grandfamilies. Their insights were an extremely valuable part of my research process.

These same community educators identified families eligible to participate in the study and then recruited them to take part in it. They described to families why I was doing the study and what their involvement would look like. Having a trusted community resource as the main point of contact for the families I interviewed was essential in creating the trust necessary for families to agree to take part in this study.

My sample consisted of grandfamilies with a youth between the ages of twelve and eighteen. It is important to note that my sample is not representative of grandfamilies in the United States or in New York State. Instead, it consists of families who had been involved with a local community agency in some way and, via that agency, were recruited to take part in the study. Some families had had very limited contact with the agency, while others were actively engaged in weekly support groups or youth activities. Although all families resided in New York State, the sample was geographically diverse, drawing from very small rural towns, midsized cities in upstate New York, urban areas outside of New York City, and New York City itself.

All interviews were conducted by me or one of my two research assistants. We conducted our interviews at each local community agency, doing our data collection in the evening when children were out of school and providing families with dinner while they took part in the study. In the first stage of the data-collection process, the teenager was given a survey to complete on a computer, while the grandparent was given a survey that was read out loud by the interviewer and filled in based on the grandparents' responses (we took this approach due to some literacy and vision concerns about the grandparents as well as to create a rapport between ourselves and the grandparents). Both the grandparent and grandchild surveys asked questions about household living arrangements and family background as well as about the parenting behaviors of the grandparent, how the grandparent and youth interacted together, and the youth's behavior and progress in school.

The central part of the study occurred next, when we videotaped the youth and grandparent talking for twenty minutes. Using index cards, we gave the families conversational prompts and asked them to talk just as they would if they were in their own homes, leaving the room while they did so. Going through the index cards, families were prompted to talk about two topics. First, the grandparent was asked to respond to and discuss with the grandchild the following questions: What is life like for a grandparent raising a grandchild? What are the best things, and what are the hardest things? Next, the grandchild was asked to respond to and discuss the exact same questions from his perspective. Then, the grandchild was asked to identify a specific topic on which he and his grandparent disagreed. We encouraged both sides to present their views on the topic and to attempt to come to a resolution. Finally, the grandparent chose her own topic of disagreement and a similar discussion took part. Each of the four segments was timed to last five minutes, with the interviewer coming back into the room at the end of each segment to move the family on to the next topic.

At the end of the four video segments, the teenager was sent to a different room, while the grandparent stayed behind to answer some open-ended questions that were of a more sensitive and complex nature. We asked the grandparent to tell us the story of how the youth came to live with him or her, stories that were often painful and complex. We also asked the grandparents to tell us about the extent of their contact with the children's parents as well the nature of those interactions, when they occur. Finally, we asked the grandparents to reflect on their parenting practices, especially how parenting has changed or stayed the same compared to when they were raising their children the first time around. Both grandparents and youths were paid for taking part in the study. Detailed information about the surveys, video protocol, and open-ended interviews are provided in the appendix.

While a few grandparents, and a few more youths, were a bit reluctant to talk about their family lives on camera, most eagerly embraced the opportunity not only to tell us their stories but also to sit down and communicate with each other. For the most part, grandparents and grandchildren quickly warmed up to the task and appeared to talk with each other as if there was no video camera in the room, as evidenced by the humor, occasional off-color comment, heated discussions, and even tears. More than one grandparent commented at the end of the study that they and their grandchildren talked about things in this interview that they had never discussed before and that they really appreciated the chance to hear their grandchildren's perspective. As those in any busy family can imagine, having the chance to take a break from the usual routine and discuss big-picture questions was, for many, a refreshing experience.

Video data capturing interactions between grandparents and grandchildren as they discussed our prompts are a particularly unique and important feature of this study. No other study of grandfamilies has gathered this type of information. Such data are crucial in order to achieve the key goal of the study—to get "under the roof" of grandfamily households and understand the nuanced relationships occurring there. Once all the interviews were done, we set ourselves to the task of systematically categorizing, or coding, those data. My research team watched each video multiple times and, using a rigorous coding system (the details of which are available in the appendix), gave each grandparent and grandchild a numerical score (ranging from one to nine) on dimensions such as anger, depression, listener responsiveness, and communication. We also scored grandparent-specific behaviors such as the use of inductive reasoning when talking with the teen as well as teenager-specific behaviors such as maturity. Finally, we gave the grandparent–grandchild pair a score for overall relationship quality, based on our observations of their conversation together. This careful observation and coding of videotaped grandparent–grandchild interactions provides an excellent opportunity to measure relationships in grandfamilies.

I combine video data with information from the grandparent and grandchild surveys. I also include information gathered from the open-ended interviews of the grandparents as well as transcripts from the video observations. Each interview and video was transcribed and entered into a database. My research team and I read through a set of transcripts, went through an inductive process of determining themes related to the key concepts of interest in the study, and then coded the rest of the transcripts for these themes. The themes we looked for in the transcripts and coded include the role of the grandparent in the youth's life, parenting behaviors, how the grandparent and youth view the parent, health concerns, and legal issues (see appendix for details on how this information was coded).

While most research projects utilize just one data-collection method, this project takes a multimethod approach. I chose the three research approaches used in this project—video, surveys, and qualitative interviews—because they have complementary strengths. Surveys allow me to ask a large number of questions covering a wide range of topics, utilizing multiple questions to capture many aspects of the same phenomenon, such as family routines. The survey questions used in this study were drawn from existing, nationally representative surveys of youths and families and therefore also allow for a comparison between the families in this study and those of the larger U.S. population. The video data give me a chance to carefully examine the interpersonal relationships and interactions between grandparents and the grandchildren they are raising. Rather than simply asking grandparents and teenagers how well they get along or asking teenagers to report how angry or happy they feel, the videos allow me to actually observe their relationship and behaviors while discussing potentially challenging topics. The verbal and nonverbal expressions of love, happiness, frustration, and anger conveyed in the videos provide invaluable information about how teenagers and grandparents feel as they discuss their families and relationships. Finally, the open-ended interview questions give me a chance to examine topics that are too nuanced to be captured on a survey, such as how the youths and grandparents perceive the parents' roles within the family. Bringing all three of these approaches together makes my study much richer than it would be had I used only one method.

Throughout the book, I also draw upon information from other, larger datasets to enhance our understanding of grandfamilies and to put my findings in context. These data contain information on a broad set of grandfamilies, including children interviewed starting from birth and followed through adolescence. Combining the nuanced insights from my New York data with the information from these larger and broader samples allows for a more in-depth understanding of grandfamilies than would be obtained from focusing on just one data source alone.

Description of Sample

Table I.3 provides information about the fifty-nine families in this study. As this table indicates, the vast majority (81 percent) of the grandparents interviewed were grandmothers. At the time of the study, the grandparents' average age was sixty-three years old, and the teenagers averaged fifteen years old. A total of 26 percent of the children in the study were non-Hispanic African American, 46 percent were non-Hispanic white, and 15 percent were Hispanic. Just under half of the grandparents were married, and their average level of education was twelve years. Notably, children in the sample had been living with their grandparents for a long time—ten years on average—and only 7 percent of the sample came to live with their grandparents in the past year.

Comparing the description of the New York sample in table I.3 with that of the representative sample of U.S. grandfamilies in tables I.1 and I.2 illustrates that in terms of racial and ethnic breakdown, grandparent marital status, and grandparent education, the New York sample examined in

TABLE I.3. Description of New York sample

VARIABLE	MEAN OR PERCENT
Grandparent is maternal grandmother	47%
Grandparent is paternal grandmother	34%
Grandparent is maternal grandfather	7%
Grandparent other relationship (e.g., great-grandmother)	12%
Grandparent age	63 years old
Youth age	15 years old
Youth is male	33%
Youth is African American, non-Hispanic	26%
Youth is Hispanic	15%
Youth is white, non-Hispanic	42%
Youth is other race	13%
Years youth has lived with grandparent	10 years
Youth has lived with grandparent for 10 or more years	56%
Age youth arrived in grandparent household	5 years old
Youth has siblings outside of household	80%
Youth has siblings living with a parent	50%
Grandparent married	47%
Grandparent has less than high school education	19%
Grandparent has high school degree	41%
Grandparent has some college	31%
Grandparent is college graduate	9%
Grandparent is employed	24%
Grandparent has a disability	32%
Youth has a health condition (n = 41)	51%

this study closely approximates the national sample of grand-families. The New York sample does differ from the larger U.S. sample in that grandparents in the New York sample are less likely to be employed (24 percent employed) and more likely to have a disability (32 percent report a disability).

Family Stories

In this section, I describe the situations of five families chosen for elaboration because their stories, as well as that of Lucille and Lindsey, discussed previously, represent themes occurring throughout the study. While each family is unique, these exemplar families' stories include common threads experienced by others in the study, and therefore, I elaborate on their lives more fully in order to shed light on the variety of experiences found in the grandfamilies I interviewed. Throughout the book, I will refer back to these exemplar families. I will also present information from interviews with the numerous other families in the study. Here and elsewhere in the book, all names have been changed. Table I.4 provides information about these six exemplar families.

ANDREA AND MONICA

Monica took in her granddaughter, Andrea, when Andrea was just under two years old. Her father, Jamal, was incarcerated, and Andrea's mother, Monique, had asked Monica to care for Andrea while she went to school in another state. As it turned out, Monique never went to school, yet never came back to claim her daughter. Monique now lives nearby with her current husband and their children. Despite living nearby, Monique sees Andrea, now age twelve, only sporadically. Perhaps surprisingly, Andrea has a closer relationship with her father, despite the fact that he remains incarcerated. Andrea talks on the phone with him several times a week

TABLE I.4. Description of exemplar families

GRANDCHILD NAME	GRANDCHILD AGE	GRANDPARENT NAME	GRANDPARENT AGE	OTHER FAMILY MEMBERS	LENGTH IN GRANDFAMILY
Lindsey	16 years old	Lucille	74 years old	Mother: Angie	13 years
Andrea	12 years old	Monica	53 years old	Father: Jamal Mother: Monique	11 years
Adam	15 years old	Betty	63 years old	Father: Lance Mother: Janet	12 years
Ashley	15 years old	Nancy	71 years old	Grandfather: Frank Father: Thomas Mother: Cindy	6 years
Stephen	16 years old	Bob	66 years old	Grandmother: Jeanne Mother: Carrie	1 year
Lila	12 years old	Patty	54 years old	Mother: Nina	Since birth

and visits him in person every other weekend. They have a "very strong" bond, Monica says.

Having only had one child but always wanting more, Monica "was in heaven" when Andrea came to live with her. However, she also is working hard to keep Andrea on the right path and to learn from the mistakes she feels she made when raising Jamal. Although Andrea expresses some appreciation for Monica, saying she likes "knowing somebody loves me enough to raise me," Andrea has become moody lately and has lost interest in some activities that she once enjoyed. She is also butting heads with Monica, now age fifty-three, over issues such as boys. The tension between Monica and Andrea was apparent during the video section of their interview, when they chose to discuss the topic of dating. Their conversation became so heated that each one was close to tears, and Andrea almost walked out. Wanting what is best for Andrea and concerned about their increasing battles, Monica "doesn't want the communication to close up between us" and has told Andrea that she can choose to live with her mother at any time, saying, "it would kill me to let [her] go, but if that was the only way to save [Andrea's] life, then I would do it." She fears that if they continue butting heads, Andrea will indeed leave her.

ADAM AND BETTY

Like Monica, Betty has seen some changes in her grandson Adam, age fifteen, as he entered the teenage years, noting that, among other things, Adam doesn't smile in pictures anymore. She attributes these changes to his increasing awareness of his parents' poor behavior. Betty, age sixty-three, struggles herself to balance the love she has for her son Lance with the anger she feels about what Lance has done to Adam. From the very beginning of Adam's life, "something didn't feel right" with the way that Lance and his girlfriend acted around Adam. Her fears were confirmed when, with Adam just an infant, Lance confessed that he wasn't ready to be a father and that he tried to cause a miscarriage in Adam's mother, Janet, by throwing her down the stairs during the last weeks of her pregnancy. With Lance in and out of prison, Adam and Janet lived with Betty for a while, but over time, Janet "was there less and less." Alarmed by Janet's erratic and sometimes harmful behavior toward Adam and Lance's violent tendencies, Betty eventually went to court and obtained custody of Adam. Adam has lived with her ever since. Betty finds it challenging to know how to best incorporate Adam's nearby parents into their life.

Lance cycles in and out of prison and their lives, sometimes attempting to gain custody, and is often violent. Janet reached out recently and said she wanted Adam to get to know her other children. She then abruptly cut off contact, leaving Adam devastated. Adam expresses guarded appreciation for Betty, saying with the briefest of smiles, "At least you know what you are doing . . . for the most part," while at the same time taking a cynical view of his parents, noting, "My parents were horrible, so why do I care if they're not here?" Betty agrees with a rueful laugh, saying of Lance, her son, "He just didn't fit the father bill like he should have, and he certainly wasn't there for you as he should be. . . . He just doesn't get it."

ASHLEY, NANCY, AND FRANK

Ashley, age fifteen, lives with her paternal grandparents, Nancy and Frank. Ashley's mother, Cindy, had a substance abuse problem. This led to the involvement of child protective services and, eventually, Cindy giving up all rights to Ashley when Ashley was very young. Ashley lived with her father, Thomas, for some time. However, he also struggled with substance abuse issues and later passed away. After

Thomas's death, Ashley spent some time in foster care before coming to live with Nancy and Frank. Ashley has no contact with her mother. She refers to Nancy as "Mom" and talks about how she likes the fact that they look alike and that, through Nancy, she "still has pieces" of her father with her.

At the time of our interview, Ashley had been living with Nancy and Frank for almost seven years. The two grandparents are in their late sixties and early seventies. However, the time she spent in multiple foster homes remained present in her mind, and Ashley expressed nervousness that she would end up back in foster care again, saying, "I've had so many foster care families, people trying to take care of me, and then eventually [I] just get kicked back out. That's what I'm waiting for." Nancy tries to reassure Ashley, saying, "We'll never kick you out."

Ashley and Nancy talk about fun times they have together, including traveling and going out to dinner, but also openly discuss the difficulties they face. Ashley acknowledges that her behavior can be challenging, describing some particularly tumultuous years when she first came to live with Nancy and Frank. However, she is optimistic about their future relationship, saying, "I'm still a teenager, and I'm still growing up, and there's still time to become better." Interviewed away from Ashley, Nancy laments Ashley's "defiant" attitude and the overall tone of their relationship, noting that she has less fun with Ashley than she did while raising her two sons.

STEPHEN, JEANNE, AND BOB

Unlike many other families in this study, most of whom have been living together for a long time, Stephen, age sixteen, and his grandparents are still adjusting to their new living situation. Stephen came to live with his maternal grandparents, Bob and Jeanne, who are in their midsixties, a year ago, when he was fifteen. While things are getting better, the transition has been difficult for everyone. Stephen instigated his own move to their home, calling Bob and Jeanne while they were away on vacation and asking them to take him in. According to Jeanne, the phone call did not come as a surprise. Their daughter, Carrie, and her new boyfriend were alternately fighting with Stephen or ignoring him, leaving Stephen to fend for himself most days, often missing the school bus and getting into trouble. Indeed, Stephen's home life had been difficult for a long time. Bob and Jeanne offered to take him in eight years ago, but the offer was rebuffed; they now wonder if things would be better if they had pushed the issue harder.

Stephen has a lot of anger and attitude but is also smart and funny. He has a hard time sitting still during the video interview and cracks a series of inappropriate jokes, to which Bob responds with patience and some humor. Stephen regularly goes to therapy, and Bob and Jeanne are impressed that by doing so he is addressing a lot of important issues around his parents. Bob and Jeanne are careful to avoid saying bad things about Carrie. Instead, they wait for Stephen to come to his own conclusions about her, noting that "he loves his mother dearly, but at some point, he is going to face the issue that he is mad at his mother." Jeanne struggles with her recent transition from grandmother to caretaker, saying, "I really miss being that grandmother" who spoiled Stephen. "It's sad for me. It's like a person that's been lost that I don't have anymore." At the same time, Jeanne reflects on the fact that she is a much more relaxed parent with Stephen than she was with her daughter, noting that she has a better perspective on what is important and what is not worth worrying about.

Lila, age twelve, and her maternal grandmother, Patty, fifty-four, exude love and warmth. Their video is filled with smiles and affectionate looks as they reflect with each other on how happy they are to be living together. Lila's mother, Nina (Patty's daughter), was only fifteen years old when Lila was born, and Lila came to live with her grandmother and grandfather right from the hospital. For her part, Patty is grateful for the chance to raise Lila, with whom she has a better relationship and more in common than she ever did with Nina. Patty also appreciates the fact that she is a better parent now than she was the first time around, having gained experience as well as a better sense of herself. As she notes, "I'm not busy chasing my own tail finding out who I am. I know who I am and where I want to be in my life." Lila has come to realize the benefits of being raised by her grandparents. She notes that she is better off with them than she would be with her parents and that in many ways, her upbringing is more "awesome" than some of her friends who are being raised by their own parents. Lila appreciates that her grandparents take her to visit historical sites, support her many activities, and "actually have time for me." Lila sees her mother regularly as well as her half-siblings. She thinks of her mother as an older sister who can help her download songs and offer advice on questions that are too embarrassing to ask her grandmother. Her father regularly sends gifts but is not emotionally involved with Lila. As she looks to her future and contemplates getting married one day, Lila is adamant that her grandfather will walk her down the aisle; she is not sure whether she will invite her father to the wedding.

Summary and Description of Book

The stories of these exemplar families illustrate the complexity of grandfamilies' lives. Their stories will be fleshed out with those of the other families interviewed for this book. As will be shown in chapter 1, many factors can lead a child to be raised by her grandparent. Most commonly, this is a voluntary decision on the part of the parent, as experienced by youths such as Lindsey, Andrea, and Adam. Notably, parents who voluntarily give up their children often go on to have and raise other children. This can cause the children being raised by their grandparents great pain.

Youths and grandparents in grandfamilies seek to define their roles in relation to each other. These issues are discussed in chapters 2 and 3, which explore how grandparents and teenagers, respectively, work to define their roles and identities. Some grandchildren go out of their way to refer to their grandmothers as "Mom." Others explicitly state the opposite, echoing Lindsey and saying, "This isn't my mom." At the same time, both grandparents and grandchildren express strong feelings of gratitude about the unique roles they are able to play in each other's lives. Whether it is the more cynical view of Adam, telling Betty, "You have your faults and all your problems and everything, but at least you know what you are doing, for the most part"—or as April, age fourteen, says of her grandparents, "They are there whenever you need them, they are on your side"—grandchildren in this study went above and beyond to emphasize how much they appreciate the emotional and material support provided to them by their grandparents. Grandparents themselves also appreciate the opportunity to play a special role in their grandchildren's lives and gain a sense of pride and meaning in doing so. As stated by one grandmother, "Grandparents are like a natural resource. It's like having gold."

As these stories show, children in grandfamilies often struggle to create for themselves a coherent narrative of how and why they came to live with their grandparents and what role their parents have in their lives. Despite not living in the household, parents play a key role in the lives of those in grandfamilies. Oftentimes parents live nearby and are in regular contact with their children. Chapter 4 explores the role of the absent parent, showing that issues regarding parents and their roles in the lives of grandfamilies often come to a head during the teenage years. At that time, youths, even those who have been living with their grandparents for the vast majority of their lives, may reevaluate their parents' past behavior and current involvement during this time. Some youths, like Lila, are able to incorporate their mothers into their lives in a way that works for everyone—Lila is clear about what her mother can and cannot do for her and finds that her grandmother can fill the gaps that her mother cannot. For others, such as Lindsey, the absent mother leaves a hole that cannot be filled, even by Lucille, who has raised her from an early age. In instances like this, teenagers' struggles with feelings toward their parents often spill over onto the people closest at hand—their grandparents.

Grandfamilies face numerous challenges as well. Some of these have to do with the relatively high rates of poverty and resulting strain faced by many such families. However, other challenges are unique—these include a high prevalence of health problems among both grandparents and grandchildren, the emotional and financial costs of repeated legal battles with the nonresident parents, and a generation gap that often manifests itself in grandparents struggling to understand what is and isn't appropriate in terms of parenting and modern youth behavior, particularly around technology. Several policies and programs exist to address these challenges, and chapter 5 highlights these programs as well as areas in which such interventions need to be modified or enhanced.

Chapter 6 presents information from a brief follow-up study, providing information on where the families I interviewed were three years after the study ended, allowing us to understand how the lives of the families taking part in this study evolved, especially during the critical period in which many were transitioning to adulthood.

Finally, the conclusion closes with a summary of the patterns observed in the stories of the lives of children being raised by their grandparents and a call for future work in this area.

Thanks to the generosity of the families who agreed to take part in this study, this book gives us a peek "under the roof" of grandfamilies' lives, highlighting the unique strengths as well as challenges that occur when children are raised by their grandparents. By telling the stories of the families in this study, this book not only increases our understanding of grandfamilies but also sheds light on ways in which policies and programs may be tailored or developed to address the unique situations of such households.

1

What Leads to the Formation of Grandfamilies?

When I first began studying grandfamilies, I assumed that most children entered into this living arrangement because both of their parents were unable to care for them, due to death, incarceration, or as a result of child welfare services removing the child from the parental home because of abuse or neglect. In contrast, what I discovered is that many children in grandfamilies remain in contact with their parents, especially their mothers. Their parents are not deceased, in jail, or otherwise incapacitated but instead, like Stephen's mother, Carrie, often live nearby, in some cases even raising other children. Additionally, few children come to live with their grandparents due to child welfare removing the children from the parental homes. This raises the question of what, then, leads to the formation of grandfamilies? As this chapter shows, the answer is more complex than I previously imagined.

Indeed, at the start of my research, I assumed that the families I interviewed would have clear, concise explanations for why the grandchild was no longer living with his or her parents. To capture this, I included a single question on the survey that I gave to grandparents, asking them to check boxes indicating the main reasons that their grandchildren came to live with them. It only took a few interviews for me to realize how misguided this approach was. The answer to the question of "How did your grandchild to come live with you?" was not something that could be measured by checking a box. As soon as I asked the question, grandparents would launch into very long and complicated stories. I found myself abandoning the boxes and rapidly scribbling detailed notes on the back of the survey form. After the first round of interviews, my team and I realized that in order to capture the complexity of how grandfamilies came to be, we would need to let the grandparents tell us in their own words, not try to force them into categories. Therefore, from that point forward, we simply asked grandparents to tell us the story of how their grandchildren came to live with them, turned on our recorder, and listened. This chapter presents the stories of what we heard.

Stephen's story is one example. As noted in the introduction, Stephen came to live with his grandparents Bob and Jeanne a year prior to our interview, when he called them and asked to move in. Bob and Jeanne were not that surprised. They had watched from afar as Stephen's mother, their daughter Carrie, increasingly backed away from Stephen, leaving him to fend for himself.

Stephen had become so angry and aggressive that his mother had sought help from the juvenile courts to put restrictions on Stephen and keep him in line. That, for his grandparents, was a defining reason they willingly intervened when Stephen called and asked to come live with them.

"It had gotten bad between his mother and him," Jeanne says. "It had escalated, and he was not going to school. And the majority of the time, he was missing the bus. He was getting himself up by himself in the morning, which he's never

been good at doing, and he was coming home to an empty home, empty house, and that had been going on for years."

"His personality," Bob adds, "he comes across macho and that's just a facade. . . . He was just ready to blow."

"I mean, I had to patch three holes in different doors; he put his fist through it," says Bob of Stephen's anger.

Since Stephen had come to live with them, Bob and Jeanne sought counseling for Stephen and for them. They were all learning a lot and working to deal with the trauma and anger that Stephen was feeling toward his mother.

"He loves his mother dearly," says Bob, "but I think down deep inside, if he continues to go for therapy, at some point, he is going to face the issue that he's mad at his mother. . . . There's an anger."

Stephen still sees his mother regularly, visiting her over a weekend or during holidays. His father, who has serious substance abuse issues, is not in the picture.

"We have worked very, very hard," Jeanne says, "so it would get better with his mom because I really wanted him to have a relationship with her. And now it's to the point that he usually does spend a night or two, usually the weekend over at his mom's. . . . In our opinion, he's still not his mom's priority. He likes to think he is. Or she'll pretend that he is, but she still is his mom and, you know, I so badly want that to be good for him."

The therapy is helping, his grandparents believe. But there's a long road ahead.

"He may never get everything resolved," says Bob, "but he's a much better human being now than he was a year ago, and he's much calmer and much more relaxed as a person."

This chapter explores the complex reasons that grandchildren, such as Stephen, came to leave their parental home and

moved in with their grandparents. It is important to note that my data-collection approach only allows me to get grandparents' perspectives on why children were not living with their parents. The grandparents were very clear that they did not want us to ask the grandchildren directly about their parents and why they were not living with them, as they felt it would be too upsetting. In addition, I did not interview the parents themselves. If I had, we likely would have heard a very different story of how and why their children left their homes and came to live with the grandparents.

Interviews with parents whose children do not live with them are very rare. However, the Fragile Families study mentioned in the introduction does contain information gathered from interviews of mothers whose children are living with their grandparents. Along with my colleague Natasha Pilkauskas,[1] I examined those data and compared mothers' stories of how their children came to enter grandfamily living arrangements with those of the grandparents themselves. Perhaps surprisingly, there was a great deal of similarity. Both mothers and grandparents reported that the most common reason that the grandchild came to live with the grandparent was that the parent voluntarily gave up the child or that an informal agreement was reached between the mother and grandparent (explored in more detail later in this chapter). The only area in which mothers and grandparents showed disagreement was whether the mother's substance abuse problems led to the formation of the grandfamily household; 20 percent of grandparents said this was the case, compared to only 2 percent of mothers. Thus while the Fragile Families survey did not capture entirely the same type of information as my New York study, the results suggest that, with the exception of substance abuse, mothers and grandparents generally agree on the reasons children left the parental home and came to live with their grandparents.

That said, more detailed interviews with mothers of children in grandfamilies are sorely needed to get a fuller sense of their perspective.

Going through the varied and complicated responses that the grandparents in my study reported, I was able to discern several reasons for the formation of grandfamily households. These are indicated in table 1.1, illustrating that a variety of factors are at play in the formation of grand-family households. For many children, more than one factor was mentioned as the main reason for not living with his or her parents. Additionally, the reasons children do not live with their fathers differ from the reasons they do not live with their mothers. For example, incarceration is the second most common reason that children do not live with their fathers but is quite rare when it comes to mothers. For mothers, the fact that their spouses or partners either were abusive toward or did not like the children was a relatively common reason that children came to live with their grandparents, but this was not the case for fathers. Grandparents reported that abuse and neglect were the main reasons that children were not living with their mothers but much less so for fathers. However, for only a very small number of families (12 percent) were child protective services (CPS) actually involved in removing the child from the parental home, suggesting that the grandparents' reports reflect their own assessments that abuse and neglect were taking place, rather than those of a social service agency. Finally, it is important to note that for 28 percent of the families I interviewed, grandparents had so little contact with their grandchildren's fathers, and the fathers had not been in their children's lives for so long, that they were not able to provide any information as to why a child was not living with the father.

This chapter examines patterns in the formation of grandfamily households, laying the groundwork for future chapters that consider the implications for grandparents and grandchildren alike.

Getting Shoved by the Wayside

As shown in table 1.1, the most common reason children in my study came to live with their grandparent is that the parent voluntarily gave up the child. This was cited for 38 percent of the children as a reason they were not living with their mothers and, for 33 percent, a reason they were not living with their fathers. This is not a question that we originally asked in our survey, and, indeed, other researchers have not fully captured this either. By asking grandparents in an open-ended way, we discovered that the most common reason for a child entering into a grandfamily living arrangement was something that we had never thought to ask directly.

TABLE 1.1. Reasons youth is not living with parents

	REASON NOT LIVING WITH MOTHER (%)	REASON NOT LIVING WITH FATHER (%)
Voluntarily gave up child	38	33
Substance abuse	26	12
Grandparent reports parent neglectful/abusive	26	10
Partner had issues with / abusive toward child	16	3
Deceased	10	12
Incarcerated	10	21
Too young	10	2
Mental health problems	9	—
Child protective services involved	12	—

NOTE: Multiple reasons could be cited per youth.

Shirley, age sixty-five, describes how this happened for her grandson Christopher, age seventeen. "His birth mother really signed off on him when he was four," she says, "after she and my son divorced. He went with my son for eight years, and that was just horrible. My son didn't take care of him. They had two more children, and Christopher just got shoved by the wayside. And then when he was thirteen, they just called us one Saturday night and said, 'Christopher's not going to live here anymore, come and get him, he's out.'"

Christopher, she says, is hurt over his mother's abandonment and worries about his father. He desperately wants a relationship with him, but it's not in the cards.

"So he gets angry with me, very angry and that's where we clash," she says.

Christopher's father and new wife had two children of their own—"two precious girls"—who got all of the attention, Shirley says. His father is no longer in Christopher's life.

"Never [came] to a ball game, hockey game, or lacrosse," she says. The only time Christopher's father visited was when he appeared in court during the custody hearing.

"You shouldn't have to tell your son, 'Get your fanny up here and see your son,'" she says. "But that's the reality." All of this, she says, makes her worry that Christopher's anger will lead him to the wrong friends, and that drives her protectiveness toward him.

There are a couple of noteworthy features of Christopher and Shirley's story. First, it clearly illustrates the voluntary, and even proactive, nature of the circumstances that lead children to come to live with their grandparents. In Christopher's case, his father actively initiated the move, kicking Christopher out of the home where he had been living for eight years. Second, the quotations show another common pattern regarding the complexity of grandfamilies. When parents move on to have children with other partners, they often find it difficult to integrate their existing children into their household. This leads to the situation in which children who live with their grandparents have siblings (often half-siblings) who remain with their parents. As shown in table I.2, half of the children in my study had one or more siblings, often half-siblings, who remained with their mothers or fathers. For example, as noted earlier and explored more in chapter 3, Andrea's mother left her with her grandmother Monica when she was two years old. She never went off to school, as she said she would, and also never came back for Andrea. Andrea's mother now lives nearby and is raising the children who she has had with a new partner, Andrea's half-siblings.

Another grandchild I interviewed, James, has a father who has also remarried and is more focused on his new girlfriend and her children. As shown in chapter 4, James longs for his father, even riding his bike past his father's house, hoping to be invited in. He never is.

The fact that many children not only are voluntarily given up by their parents but often live near them and in contact with them only exacerbates the hurt feelings that emerge when children see their parents living with step- or half-siblings, while they are living with their grandparents. This issue is explored more fully in chapter 4.

Missing Fathers

Another finding that emerges from table 1.1 is that, for over a quarter of children, no information was provided on the reasons they were not living with their fathers. Some of these children never knew their fathers and, therefore, have no specific stories to tell about why they are not living with them. In some cases, the father is intentionally kept out of the child's life. For example, another grandmother I interviewed,

Paula, worked hard to ensure that her grandchildren's biological father was not listed on their birth certificates; he had been incarcerated several times for child sexual abuse, and she did not want him to have any rights to contact her grandchildren.

Other children remain in touch with their fathers but hadn't lived with them prior to coming to live with their grandparents and, therefore, did not provide specific reasons they were not living with the fathers.

Among the reasons that were provided for why youths were not living with their fathers, there are some similarities and some differences compared to those provided regarding their mothers. As with mothers, the most common reason a child was not living with a father is that he had voluntarily given the child up. Unlike with mothers, the next most common reason was that the father was incarcerated (this applied to 21 percent of youths). In these situations, grandfamilies differed in how they incorporated incarcerated fathers into their lives. For Andrea, her father's incarceration does not hinder, and may even promote, her relationship with him. She holds to a regular schedule of visiting him and, according to her grandmother Monica, feels very comfortable doing so. In contrast, Betty and Adam struggle with how to incorporate Adam's father, Lance, into their lives as he cycles in and out of prison and displays very violent tendencies fueled in large part by his substance addictions. As illustrated in chapter 4, with Lance now back in prison, Adam has decided that he wants nothing to do with him.

Mothers' Partners

While grandchildren's fathers are often absent from their lives, other men can play a key role. In particular, mothers' partners at times play a negative role in the lives of children in grandfamilies. Difficulties with mothers' partners were mentioned by 16 percent of the grandparents I interviewed as a reason children in this study came to live with their grandparents.

For too many of these children, the impetus for them to leave their parental households and come to live with a grandparent had to do with abusive behavior on the part of their mothers' partners, including instances of sexual abuse. Heather (age fourteen) and her sister were living at home when their mother began a relationship with a man she met on the internet. After a time, he came to live with them and soon molested Heather's sister. After he was arrested, Heather and her sister were put in foster care until her grandparents could arrange to take them in. In the meantime, Heather's mother moved to a different state to be with the abusive man (after he was released from jail) and ended up marrying him. Despite all this, Heather misses her mother and sees her once a year during a visit that is supervised by her grandmother.

Similarly, as discussed later, Amy, age fifteen, came to live with her grandmother Justina, sixty-five, after her mother's boyfriend raped Amy's older sister. After the boyfriend was arrested, social services took Amy and her sister away from their mother. Justina went to court with her son, their father, to obtain custody of the girls, but when the father was judged to be unfit, she was granted custody. Amy sees her mother and father often, and Justina describes her as having a great relationship with her father but a very distant one with her mother.

In other cases, a mother's partner is not abusive but simply doesn't get along with the children she brings from a previous relationship. Indeed, a key reason Stephen came to live with his grandparents was that he did not get along with his mother's boyfriend. According to his grandparents Bob and Jeanne, this was the motivating factor leading Stephen to contact them and asking to move in.

Sometimes the problematic partner is the child's biological father. Thomas, David's father, showed up out of the blue one day when David was eleven. Thomas had disappeared from the life of David and his mother, Ann, early on. Thomas was on the run from authorities in a different state, where he was wanted for a violent crime, but Ann took him in, and they reunited. David's grandmother Sue was wary of Thomas's presence, but Ann was adamant that he stay. Thomas turned violent, however, and David told his grandmother that he was afraid to go home. After investigating, the police told Ann that her son could no longer live with her if Thomas was also in the house. Yet Ann chose to remain with Thomas instead of living with her son, and David's grandparents took him in, where he remains today. At the time of the interview, David's father was in prison, and his mother, with mental health issues, was cycling in and out of his life.

These stories make clear that while mothers' partners are a frequent reason children do not live with their parents, mothers sometimes choose to remain with, and have children with, those partners. This, again, leads to the quite common situation in which children are being raised by their grandparents while having half-siblings living with their parents and also reflects another type of scenario in which parents make the choice to voluntarily give up their children to the grandparents—in this case, so that they can remain with their partners.

When Child Welfare Is Involved

For a smaller number of families, child protective services played a role in the child coming to live with the grandparent.

In these families, the parent did not voluntarily give up the child. Instead, a social service agency precipitated the removal of the child from the parental home. For example, Mona, age fifty-five, took in April (age fourteen) and her sister after child protective services investigated their mother for abuse and neglect. According to Mona, April's older sister, age five at the time, was doing all the cooking and cleaning for herself and two-year-old April. Both of April's parents ended up in prison.

Leona describes how her granddaughters came to live with her, narrating how her daughter called her one day and said that CPS was about to remove the children from her home. Leona called the social service worker who told her that if she could come and get her two grandchildren before midnight, they would not have to go to foster care. "And I'm going 'are you serious? I'm working twelve-hour shifts at a factory.'" But she dropped everything and went down to the CPS office and took the children home. "But to this day," she says, her daughter "still blames me for taking the kids. She says, 'If it wasn't for you, I'd still have my kids.' I says, 'No, if it wasn't for me, they'd have been in foster care.'"

Leona got permanent custody of her two grandchildren because the children's parents could never prove to the court that they could provide a safe home for them. Their mother now has a new boyfriend and lives with him and his children. As Leona says, "She chose his kids over her kids. We're fine with it."

Similarly, Aurora, age fifty-one, took in her grandson Sean, now thirteen, in order to avoid foster care. Aurora's daughter, Zoe, had Sean when she was only sixteen years old. Zoe left Sean for several days with a stranger. When CPS was alerted, a friend got in touch with Aurora and told her about the situation. Aurora is now raising Sean and some of his many siblings. His mother is currently incarcerated and is pregnant with her seventh child.

As can be seen in table 1.1, a larger number of grandparents reported that their grandchildren were abused or neglected than reported that child protective services was involved in the youths coming to live in their homes. This is likely due to the fact that grandparents are reporting on their perceptions that the children were abused or neglected by the parents. It is possible that the level of abuse was not severe enough to merit CPS involvement, that the grandparent intervened before such involvement occurred, or that the parent and grandparent came to an agreement about what was best for the child before any social services involvement occurred.

Conclusion

This chapter shows that the reasons children come to live with their grandparents are varied and complex. A key part of this complexity is the fact that, for many children, the reasons they came to live with their grandparents have to do with their parents actively choosing to give them up, or "shoving them by the wayside." This means that it is not uncommon for children in grandfamilies to live near their parents and to see them often, leading to obvious and difficult questions of why the parent has chosen not to raise them. Some parents choose their romantic partners over their children, sometimes moving on to have children with those partners. Others are consumed by mental health and substance abuse problems that result in erratic behavior toward their children. Still others are simply too immature to focus on being a parent.

Thus the stories that families tell about how their grandfamilies came to be are not straightforward and are sometimes painful, creating challenges for youths in grandfamily households. Psychological research illustrates the importance of constructing a coherent narrative or story about our lives. Such narratives provide meaning to our experiences, creating a story that we can tell to ourselves and to others in order to bring together the events of our lives in a way that creates a sense of unity and purpose. It is during adolescence when people begin to develop their life stories or narratives. Such a story moves beyond simply recalling specific events and instead puts events together and interprets them in a coherent and meaningful way. During this process, youths tell and retell their stories to themselves and to others, revising them as they gain feedback from others and greater insight into their own lives and experiences.[2]

The construction of life stories is influenced by the families in which we live and the cultural values we hold. Youths living in grandfamilies may find it challenging to form coherent narratives that involve their families, as they have fewer available frameworks or models to rely on when developing their stories. Lindsey puts it best: "When you think of family, you think of Mom, Dad, two kids, and a dog, like a normal little happy family. And then, when you're raised by a grandparent, you're thinking 'this isn't my mom. I ain't got no dad.' Everything is so off."

Lindsey and other teenagers in grandfamilies face this struggle as they take on the key task of adolescence—forming an identity by constructing a life story. As youths age, they have more and more nuanced questions about how they came to live in a grandfamily. As described in this chapter, the very stories they tell about the ways in which their families were formed can be complicated, vague, or even painful. As described in chapter 4, the ways in which their parents are incorporated into these life stories are no less complicated. First, though, I explore how youths and grandparents define their roles within grandfamilies.

2

"I Couldn't Be Prouder to Be the Caregiver of You"

*How Do Grandparents Define
Their Roles in Grandfamilies?*

This chapter examines how grandparents raising grandchildren define their roles. Because they are neither the parents of the children they are raising nor are they acting as traditional grandparents, grandparents raising grandchildren must negotiate new terrain in defining their roles. Many mourn the loss of the ability to be a "regular" grandparent who spoils the grandchildren and then returns them to their parents at the end of the day. As Stephen's grandmother Jeanne says, reflecting on the role she used to play as the "fun" grandma, "It's sad for me. It's like a person that's been lost that I don't have anymore." Others face health limitations that make parenting and keeping up with their teenagers difficult. Still others confront financial hurdles that come with raising children in retirement on a fixed income. Most feel the sharp generational divide, both a generation gap and the fact that parenting trends and behaviors are different now than when they parented the first time around.

This chapter goes into detail about the roles of grandparents in grandfamilies from the perspectives of those grandparents themselves. While grandparents raise many challenges pertaining to their role, they also highlight numerous benefits that they derive from playing such a crucial part in the lives of their grandchildren. Therefore, this chapter also focuses on an obvious, but sometimes underexplored, aspect of grandfamilies: their numerous strengths. In interviewing the families who generously agreed to take part in my study, I was repeatedly and completely amazed by the love, warmth, and commitment that came through in their interactions. In many ways, grandfamilies demonstrate the power of love to overcome trauma, disappointment, deprivation, and loss. As such, they can serve as excellent role models to us all. Indeed, I benefitted greatly from my interviews with grandparents and grandchildren. Their stories of love overcoming loss led me to consider anew how I relate to and appreciate the important people in my life. Drawing on all this complexity, this chapter illustrates the highs and lows of grandparenting in a grandfamily.

This chapter begins with the challenges facing grandfamilies and ends with the numerous rewards. Indeed, grandparents raising their grandchildren identify several advantages of their role. Many appreciate that raising their grandchildren gives them both companionship and purpose in life, feeling a strong sense of pride in the important role they are playing not only in keeping their family together but also in society at large. As one grandmother stated, "Grandparents are a natural resource. It's like having gold in front of your face."

Grandparents' roles in grandfamilies are inherently complex because our society lacks guidelines about how a grandparent raising a grandchild should behave or even what such a person should be called. As I will show later in this chapter, the issue of what grandchildren call their grandparents sits at the core of many discussions about the grandparents' role in the children's lives. In this way, grandparents in grandfamilies face challenges similar to those of stepparents. According to family researchers,[1] family relationships work best when roles within families are clearly defined and well known. For example, our society has clearly defined roles, or scripts, for "parent" and "child," with broadly agreed-upon notions of how people in each of these roles typically behave. When individuals fall outside of these socially accepted and scripted roles, tensions can emerge.

One example of this lack of role clarity can be found by looking at stepparents. Researchers describe the uncertainty felt by stepparents regarding their roles, rights, and obligations as well as a lack of clarity regarding what they should be called.[2] Stepparents, for example, often face confusion about whether they should take on a disciplinary role, a distant one, or a friendlike role with the child living in their household. Stepparents also may be uncertain about what they should be called; "Dad" may not seem right, using a first name may seem uncomfortable, and the more formal "Mr. Jones" is even less natural. The ambiguous role of stepparents is exacerbated by the fact that they often do not have any legal rights regarding their stepchildren, despite being highly involved with them. Finally, research on stepfamilies shows that a lack of certainty in the roles individuals play is greatest when people living outside of the household continue to be highly involved in family life. For example, children who live with their stepmothers and whose biological mothers live outside of the household often report having a difficult time forming a strong relationship with their stepmothers and experience torn loyalties between their stepmothers and nonresident biological mothers.

This line of research has many applications to the understanding of grandfamilies. As described later in this chapter, individuals in grandfamilies struggle to find words to describe their relationships—*parent* is not accurate, but *grandparent* doesn't seem to capture the true relationship. Lacking the very words needed to describe a relationship can present challenges to the relationship itself. In addition, as seen in the previous chapter, nonresident parents remain highly involved in the lives of grandfamilies. Their involvement can hinder the grandparents' ability to truly take on a parental role in the lives of the children they are raising, creating challenges.

Grandparents' Role in the Formation of the Grandfamily

Understanding how grandparents view themselves in their grandfamilies requires an understanding of how they interpret their role in the formation of the grandfamily itself. Chapter 1 discussed the reasons youths came to live with their grandparents. Here I focus on what role the grandparents feel they played in that process—whether they were simply reacting to circumstances or whether they actively sought out their grandchild, for example. This interpretation helps shape the feelings that grandparents have about their living situation, as explored further later in the chapter.

Some grandparents describe a very reactive role in the formation of their grandfamilies. For example, Tara's grandfather John, age sixty-six, describes the situation as something that fell into his lap and over which he really had no choice: "Tara was twenty-six months old. Her mother came to our door, and she gave us a choice: either take her on the spot—she had a little bag—or she was taking Tara and the little bag and dropping both off at social services. So it required an instant decision. It was dumped in our lap."

John says his stepdaughter, Tara's mother, was irresponsible and not ready for parenthood. She wasn't sure who the father was, and there were rumors that her current boyfriend was sexually abusing Tara.

"Tara's mother is not—I don't think that she's capable of raising Tara. She's a person that to this very day, she does things that harm herself," John says. Within the last nine years, Tara's mother has visited only twice since John and his wife moved away to a different town.

A short while after his stepdaughter dropped Tara off, John and his wife sought custody of Tara, which the judge granted. "We really didn't have a choice," says John of the custody decision, "and it changed my life completely, in some ways positively."

Similarly, Paula describes going to the hospital one day, only to unexpectedly "come home with another baby," her granddaughter Erin. Previously, Paula's daughter had given birth to a baby at age fourteen, a child whom Paula gained custody of almost immediately. Five years later, Paula's daughter had a second girl, Erin, and was unable to care for her. After being born, Erin remained in the hospital. When Paula went to visit her, she ended up bringing Erin home to stay.

Cathy, who only recently started raising her granddaughter, Holly, age eighteen, went to court during a custody battle between Holly's parents. The custody battle got so heated that the judge turned away from giving either parent custody and asked Cathy if she could take Holly instead. "I kind of just at that spot made that decision to put in for custody," Cathy says.

Much more often than this type of reactive response, though, grandparents describe taking on a proactive role in the formation of their grandfamilies. They intervened to help their grandchildren, despite the hurdles, their age, their health, and their situations in life. As Susanna puts it: "As a grandparent raising grandchildren, it's not easy, but I did it out of love. I did it out of concern. And I did it because I knew it was mine and I had to do it."

Susanna, age seventy-three, is Jordan's great-grandmother. Jordan's mother, Leila, lost custody of him and his older brother early on. Their grandmother, Susanna's daughter, was "out on the street and unable to care for them," says Susanna. Susanna had raised Leila as well, and Susanna believes that Leila abandoned Jordan, now fifteen years old, and his brother because she, too, was hurt from having her mother abandon her.

"She don't come around like she should," Susanna says of Jordan's mother. "A lot of time[s], him and his mother, they hurt because, you know, they feel like they don't have nobody but me."

Grandparents like Susanna feel strongly that raising a grandchild is their responsibility but that it also comes from a place of not just responsibility but love: "None of my daughters, like they say, want their grandchildren, you know. So, it was up to me."

Jordan is thankful for that love. As he says to Susanna, "My mom's not really in my life. My dad's not in my life. My grandmother's not in my life. It's my great-grandmother that is raising me and my older brother. Without you, me and him both probably wouldn't even know our family right now."

A key part of the proactive nature of many grandparents' roles in the formation of their grandfamilies comes from a strong desire to keep their grandchildren out of foster care, or "the system." Many grandparents feel as strongly as Joanne, saying that keeping their grandchildren out of the system is worth any kind of hardship that may come with it.

Joanne, age fifty-seven, is raising her granddaughter Rebecca, age thirteen, and Rebecca's two older sisters. Their mother is in and out of rehab, unable or unwilling to kick her drug habit, says Joanne. She lives two doors down from Joanne and the children but visits only "when she wants to eat or use my phone," Joanne says. Joanne is frustrated with her daughter, angry that she is not willing to stop using drugs and take care of her children.

"I know what I was like, you know, as a mother bringing my kids up. I know my problem was the drinking, but I was always there for my children. I never left them. To have three kids and want to keep doing drugs and not even care. If it wasn't for me and my old man, they would have been put in the system, and I grew up in the system. Never allowed to do anything. Being shipped from home to home. Never had anything. I try to give them everything I can possibly give them," she says. "My grandchildren are not going in the system. No matter how much they give me a hard time with this, they are not going in the system. I can't have it."

Other grandparents echo this sentiment, noting that the challenges of raising a grandchild cannot be denied but that they are outweighed by the need to keep their grandchildren out of the system as well as the pride that comes from being able to do so. Says Marsha, sixty-eight, of raising her great-granddaughter, Stacy, eighteen, "Ain't no easy thing. But I rather for me to get them than for them to go into the system." Like Susanna, Marsha had raised not only Anne but Anne's mother, LaToya. She had adopted LaToya after LaToya's mother, Colleen, had "got on drugs," Marsha says. LaToya was living with Marsha when Stacy was born. Later, Marsha says, when LaToya was ready to move out,

Stacy had asked to stay on with her grandmother "through elementary school. Then when she finish elementary, she said, 'Can I still stay with you until I finish junior high?'" Stacy would stay on through high school. Her relationship with her own mother is good, says Marsha, "She goes home to her mother on the weekends and whatever, but she likes staying with me."

As we saw in chapter 1, the circumstances that lead to the formation of grandfamilies include some very difficult events, such as drug addiction, death, abuse, and incarceration, all extremely trying circumstances for families to get through. Some grandparents took a proactive role as a way to find strength and meaning in the midst of the traumatic events that led to their grandchildren's removal from their homes. As Darla, whose daughter was murdered, says, "It was like I had to put grieving for my daughter on the back burner because the closest thing to my daughter was her kids, and I wanted to make sure I got them."

Darla's daughter was twenty-five when she was murdered, and Danielle, age four at the time, along with her older brother, came to live with Darla. "My life has changed quite a bit, but believe me, I wouldn't have it any other way," says Darla. Danielle is now fourteen.

Grandparents view their new role in a variety of ways. As I outline here, there are challenges in this new role as well as rewards. Raising grandchildren when they thought they would be retired and child-free is one key challenge.

"You Are My Life, but I Need My Own, Too"

Raising a grandchild, says Amy's grandmother Justina, is "not what I thought I'd be doing in a million years. It never occurred to me that I'd have to go through being a parent again at this stage."

Family research describes the challenges individuals face when their lives do not follow the timelines and phases that are considered "normal" in our society.[3] Most of us have a shared concept of a typical "life course," consisting of predictable, clearly defined events occurring at certain ages and in a certain order: childhood, adolescence, worker, parent, and grandparent. The idea of a life course gives us a sense of what to expect and how to behave during different times of our lives, as well as a series of experiences that we share with others going through similar phases at the same time.[4] The later stages of the life course are times when many people enter into retirement and cease full-time employment. For many this means time to travel, pursue hobbies or volunteer activities, perhaps take on a part-time job in a new field, and generally to have more personal time. Many become grandparents later in life and often spend significant time with their grandchildren, which is just one of many activities they may enjoy during their retirement years.

The experience of being "off time," or undergoing an event at a stage in the life course when it is not common, can be stressful and may also isolate a person from those around them. For example, grandparents raising grandchildren no longer have as much in common with their friends who are "typical" grandparents, those who hand their grandchildren back to their parents at the end of a fun day. Grandparents in grandfamilies may struggle with the fact that they do not fit with our societal image of what a "grandparent" is or with what their peers are doing in their later years. Older adulthood is typically a time when people have the freedom to explore other paths for themselves, since they are often unconstrained by the roles of parent and worker. Grandparents raising grandchildren are not able to do this. Indeed, a key developmental goal of later adulthood is being freed from the constraints of work and parenthood and gaining the ability to explore and develop other parts of oneself. It is also a time when empty nesters can feel comfort and pride in the fact that they have successfully "launched" their children. For grandparents raising grandchildren, these feelings of having successfully raised their children and of being able to take the time to focus on themselves are derailed. It is often the fact that their children are not "launched" that leads them to take on the role of raising their grandchildren in the first place.

Additionally, because many grandparents begin raising their grandchildren when the grandchildren are very young, there can be very little to no gap between the conclusion of the parenting years, with all their intensity and demands, and the start of the grandfamily years. This means that grandparents may spend decades of uninterrupted time as full-time caregivers. While doing so can be incredibly rewarding and create a sense of purpose, taking on the duties of raising children with no break can be exhausting and relentless.

While their friends are traveling or reconnecting with their spouses during retirement, grandparents raising grandchildren are thrust back into the parenting role, going to school events, keeping their grandchildren on track, and worrying about their futures. Due to the financial strain of raising grandchildren, some may not be able to retire as planned. The circumstance that many grandparents raising grandchildren face—that of being "off time"—can cause confusion and distress. One reason is that life events that occur "off time" are typically unexpected. As a result, those going through them have not had the opportunity to prepare for them, either physically (such as preparing a home for the arrival of a grandchild or saving enough money to support a larger family) or emotionally. The emotional distress can come when the image one has in her mind of what "being a grandparent" looks like differs from what her own experience is of being a grandparent. This sense of being unprepared, confused, or distressed may be especially pronounced when it is someone else's behavior that leads to the feeling of being "off time," meaning that the situation can be perceived as being outside of one's own control. For grandparents in grandfamilies, it is the behaviors and choices of others, their children, which led them to take on the role of caregiver. While many grandparents were proactive in taking on the role of caregiver and greatly appreciated the benefits of doing so, none started out thinking that this is something that they would do. Additionally, because the lives of family members are interconnected, one person's situation can affect others. In the case of grandfamilies, the other grandchildren who aren't being raised by the grandparent may get less attention, which could cause jealousy and potentially damage other grandparent–grandchild relationships.

The way people think about the "typical" life course varies by factors such as gender, race, and ethnicity. Researchers note that there is a long-standing historical pattern in which African American grandparents, particularly grandmothers, have played an important role in providing care for their grandchildren.[5] Throughout U.S. history, African American grandparents have stepped in to serve in a parental role in response to economic hardships, changes in family life, historical events, and other situations, often serving in positions of authority within a family and playing a crucial role as a linchpin in maintaining family ties. This suggests that there may be a stronger expectation for African American grandparents to be highly involved and hands-on in their grandchildren's lives. Indeed, in the United States as a whole, black children are twice as likely to live in a grandfamily as white children. These patterns suggest that African American grandparents in grandfamilies, particularly grandmothers, may experience greater social support and less of a sensation of being "off time" than others.[6] While my study contained a diverse sample, it is not large enough to allow for a systematic examination of how race or ethnicity influences how grandparents and grandchildren experience their roles in grandfamilies.

However, while taking on a parenting role may be more normative in certain communities, this does not mean it is without challenges. In her groundbreaking ethnographic work in this area, Linda Burton describes both the rewards and challenges faced by African American grandparents providing care for their grandchildren.[7] Those challenges mirror those found in my study: financial strain, lack of personal time, being pulled in too many directions, and a general feeling of being overwhelmed by numerous responsibilities. Numerous rewards to such work were also revealed, again consistent with what I found in my study, including the chance to parent again, this time with more knowledge and maturity; the companionship and love provided by grandchildren; and the feeling of satisfaction that comes from playing an important role in the lives of their grandchildren.

For some grandparents, raising grandchildren at a time when they were not expecting to means that important aspects of their lives have changed since raising their own children. For Lucille (Lindsey's great-grandmother), an important change is that she is no longer married due to the death of her husband, making the parenting role more difficult. She says, "I felt like with my boys I did a pretty good job, but I had a husband to help me. That makes a difference. Two parents makes a difference."

For other grandparents, shelving plans to retire, play golf, move to Florida, and just relax is disappointing. Elaine's husband, who is older than she is, is not happy about raising children again. "He's been there, done that," she says. "He raised his children, my children, and now he says, 'I never wanted to be faced with raising grandchildren.' He wanted to retire in Florida, so he's a very unhappy man."

Other couples find it challenging to incorporate the often-unexpected grandchild into their relationship, particularly when one partner is not the grandchild's biological grandparent, as in the case of Bo.

Bo, aged sixty-eight, is Patricia's second husband. Patricia, age sixty, took in her two grandchildren, Jennifer and Anthony—twelve and ten years old, respectively—three years earlier. Jennifer is a warm and friendly girl, but when she arrived, there were tensions, and she and her stepgrandfather, Bo, knocked heads a few times. Bo likes things a certain way, says her grandmother, and the sudden disruption of routines was difficult. Patricia runs interference and tries to limit the chaos by keeping an eye on Jennifer and her friends. Unlike when she raised her own children, for example, she prefers that Jennifer stay overnight with her friends rather than having them come to her house, mainly to keep Jennifer out of Bo's hair. "When I had a home, the kids were always staying over at my house," she says, "but because I don't own the home now, it's a little different. So I give Jennifer a little bit more leeway to stay overnight because I know that it's Bo's house."

Patricia also tries to sidestep arguments over Jennifer's use of the computer. Bo would be watching television, she says, and Jennifer would burst in and say, "Oh, I gotta get on the computer. I have to get on the computer."

"So I told you," she says to Jennifer during their dialogue, "if he's sitting there watching TV, wait a while, see what he's going to do, and then ask his permission. Because the thing is . . . he owns the house. In his mind, he feels he's being pushed out because we're three in number and we're taking over the house."

"The house is so small," Patricia says, after considering the options for Jennifer's computer use, "that it's best that he doesn't see you constantly on the computer. That's going to aggravate him."

With a dedicated desk for the computer, Patricia tells Jennifer, "then we could keep away from him for a little while. You know what I mean? I mean, everybody has their little space. . . . Doesn't it make life easier?"

"I just don't want to move," Jennifer says, worried that Bo will want her and Patricia to move out.

"I know, but if you get along and you do the right thing and you respect him, we don't have to move," responds Patricia.

"He's a tough cookie!" Jennifer says.

Patricia agrees, "He's a tough cookie, yeah. But you have to know how to get around him. He's a pussycat."

Patricia has been with Bo twenty-five years and has learned to work around his impatience. But not all the relationships last. Darla's relationship broke up when she decided to raise her grandchildren after their mother was murdered.

"It's been a very, very difficult," she says. "Once I made the decision to raise my grandchildren, my partner and I separated. I gave up a lot, but again, I wouldn't change it."

"I'm Not a Bank": Financial Challenges

Many grandparents face financial challenges in raising their grandchildren at an older age. Raising a child is expensive, and most grandparents are living on limited means in retirement. In addition, grandparents in this study and elsewhere are more likely to come from circumscribed situations. As noted in the introduction, grandfamily households are more likely to be poor or near-poor than the average U.S. household, with two-thirds of grandfamilies in the United States living at or near the federal poverty line. Yet as discussed in chapter 5, there are relatively few programs to alleviate the financial strain for grandparents raising grandchildren. In addition, support often hinges on the type of legal arrangements the children are living under.

The financial hardship that raising children at this stage of life brings is difficult for many, though few grandparents let that alter their decisions.

Brittany had been living with her grandmother Edie, age seventy-three, for thirteen years in an informal arrangement. Edie's daughter was emotionally unstable and drinking heavily. She had told Edie that she would commit suicide if Edie ever tried to get custody of Brittany, though she herself showed no signs of taking care of her. After years of not seeking formal custody of Brittany through the court system, Edie overcame her long-held fear that her daughter would harm herself and sought custody.

"I didn't want to hurt my daughter," she says, "but I couldn't take it no more because I needed support, and things are very hard because I'm on a fixed income."

To her surprise, "my daughter gave her up just like that," though Edie didn't tell Brittany that, she says, "because I don't want her to know."

With custody came some financial support from the state, which helps. "I try to make Brittany as happy as possible," she says. "You hear her, how she says, 'I want, I want, I want,' but I try to do the best I can."

While Edie is happy to have custody for the financial relief it brings, there is no joy in it, she says.

"I really miss my daughter. I love my daughter. This year in July, she turns fifty, and it hurts," says Edie. She has not spoken with her daughter for eleven years, she says.

Beyond the costs of raising a child today, grandparents face legal costs in fighting for custody. Molly and her husband sought custody of Erica after her mother abandoned her and their son, Erica's father, showed no signs of being a committed father.

"We spent thousands upon thousands of dollars fighting her [her daughter-in-law] and my son," Molly says. To add injury to insult, she says, while they were forced to spend their own savings, Erica's parents "wound up getting all this legal aid."

"We didn't ask for any money because we weren't looking for money when we took her," Molly says. "We wanted her just to have a stable home." But they struggled financially. "We don't have a lot of money," she says. "The few times that we did ask for money, we were denied by her parents."

But the bills added up. Molly was afraid that if she asked for money, the courts would take Erica away from them "because the laws, it seems, just don't work with the child; they don't care about the child."

It would take some time, but "one day we just asked her parents for some money for her orthodontist bill, and I just finally got really upset, and I said, 'Enough is enough,'" says Molly.

As any parent will tell you, it's very expensive to raise a child. And the fact that grandparents are retired, often on a fixed income, "makes it challenging. We have to plan," says Tara's grandmother. Grandchildren, like most teens, want to go to concerts and movies, they want to shop and buy the latest fashion, and they want to go out with their friends, on top of the school fees and summer camps and after-school activities.

"They're not easy," says Estelle, of her grandson Michael, age fourteen, "especially when it comes to a boy. He wants to wear something that I cannot afford, like expensive sneakers and designer clothes and I tell him, you know, with what I get, there's not a lot that I can afford. He have to wait until like four more months."

Girls are expensive too. Brittany tells her grandmother that she wants to go to a movie and a concert and shopping and travel. "You want too much, baby," Edie replies. "I told you, I'm not a bank."

In chapter 5, I discuss existing policies and policy proposals that attempt to address the financial difficulties faced by many grandfamilies.

Health Issues

For some grandparents, the challenges of raising a grandchild at an older age also include dealing with health limitations. As shown in table I.2, 32 percent of the grandparents I interviewed had a disability, such as John.

John was an executive in sales and traveled extensively when he was raising his own children, but when his stepgranddaughter, Tara, came to live with them when she was two, he had just retired because of a disability. "I retired on Social Security disability in January, and Tara came to us in May," he says.

John's stepdaughter was a troubled soul, addicted to drugs and hanging out with all the wrong people. "I mean we're talking about the kind of people that when you see them you instinctively walk on the other side of the street because of their demeanor," John says. "In our case, it [custody] was dumped in our lap." As noted earlier, Tara's mother gave them an ultimatum—take her or I'll drop her at social services: "We really didn't have a choice, and it changed my life completely, in some ways positively."

While being home allowed him to "be there for her full-time," he also felt the limitations of his health. When asked what the hardest thing about being a grandparent is, he replies, "Getting old. Because I wish that I was younger, so that I could do more of the things and have better health."

"The thing that's very, very disappointing to me," he continues, "is that I don't have the strength and the abilities that I had when I was younger. I can't really run or hike with the child like I was able to. I can't really take a bicycle trip with her, and that makes me sad because I wish my wife and I could do more. We're limited, but we're just doing the best we can."

Paula, at age sixty-one, has congestive heart failure, which leaves her both weak and worried. She is frequently laid up on the couch, which also worries her granddaughter, Erin, who is now fifteen. After a recent episode, Paula's physician changed her medication, which is helping, but the future is always on her mind. She has made provisions for Erin should she die and tries to reassure Erin that all will be well, but Erin of course remains concerned that her grandmother, whom she loves and who is her only caregiver, faces such severe health problems. "So don't worry about me being sick," she tells Erin in the interview. "I'm going to be here. OK?"

Others are not disabled but still struggle with the health challenges that come with age. As Christine, who is fifty-four, tells her twelve-year-old grandson, Joshua, "[When] I'm hurting, I still have to cook. I still have to make sure you have clean clothes. When I'm not feeling well, it's an extra effort for me." Joshua agrees, saying, "You're slow. You won't wake up in the morning." Melissa's grandmother Sherrie, at sixty-seven, has noticed a decline in her ability to take part in activities with her grandchildren, saying, "When the kids first came, we did a lot of things, but now, getting into my sixties, it's hard to keep up with the teenagers with things like roller skating and ice skating and different things that we used to do together." Jennifer talks excitedly about plans for her birthday, which include perhaps a Broadway show or a trip to a large popular mall for shopping. "I would have to call and find out," says her grandmother hesitantly. "Because that's a big mall for me to walk. But that's all right. I can sit down."

Generation Gap

In addition to health limitations, a generation gap can impact the grandparent–grandchild relationship. The way that teenagers feel about this gap is discussed in more detail in the next chapter, particularly as it relates to grandparents' understanding of the technology that plays such a big part of their grandchildren's lives. Justina, who was sixty-five at the time of our conversation, recognizes how the generation gap has the potential to influence her relationship with Amy.

"There's a big gap between the awareness of the current social event or social situation that people in their thirties who have teenage children would be more aware of, and that's one of the drawbacks. That's one disadvantage of being a grandparent raising a grandchild is you're sort of like in a different dimension. You begin to wonder, am I doing the kids a disservice or am I being overprotective? You know, I'm not sure," says Justina.

Speaking of technology, Molly notes the challenges of keeping her granddaughter safe on the computer, saying, "They didn't have all the technology when I was raising my children that they have now. You could have kept them under more control. Now they're on that internet, and you don't know what they are doing. I can't even figure out how to turn it on to figure out what they're doing. My husband did put some kind of a guard on it. Well, she figured it was on there, and she took it off."

Another challenge is the age gap between grandparents and other parents raising teens.

Shirley keeps a tight leash on her grandson Christopher worried that he will fall in with the wrong crowd. It was easier, she says, when she was raising her children because they lived on a farm, and her children couldn't just hang out as Christopher does with his friends at a local fast-food spot. Her worry is compounded because the age difference means that she doesn't know his friends' parents. "I didn't know any parents of teenagers, so it's taken all this time to get to know them," she says. "It's taken us four years because we're so much older."

Another challenge related to the generation gap is many grandparents' feeling that society has changed since they raised their children the first time around. Susanna, Jordan's great-grandmother, not only is raising Jordan but raised Jordan's mother as well. Today, she says, raising children is more difficult because they don't listen as much and have less respect for their elders.

"Back then you could tell a child something, you know, they might not listen as they should, but they would do it," she says. "With my children, I could say, 'Don't do this, do this,' and they would do it. You know, they listen. They had their chores. They know what they had to do; they did it."

She also had more authority, she felt, when she was raising her kids, mainly because she could spank them. "But now you can't do these things, so that make[s] a lot of bad kids," she says. Kids today, she believes, have the upper hand: "They say, 'We'll call the cops, we'll do this.' That made a lot of kids, well, the boss."

Life Disrupted

Finally, grandparents describe how they have had to rearrange their lives in order to raise their grandchildren. Lila's grandmother Patty tells her, "You are my life, but I need my own, too." Barbara, Stephanie's grandmother, feels the same way. Barbara was fifty-five at the time of the interview, a few years away from retirement yet but in that decade of beginning to think about it. "It's really rough," she says, "because you don't have your free time. You know, this is your time of life where you should be enjoying yourself and being out with a lot of friends and being able to do whatever you want to, and you can't do it because you can't afford a sitter."

Men in particular seemed affected by the transition into a grandfamily. As noted previously, Darla's partner chose to leave after Danielle and Anton came to stay with Darla. Stephen's grandfather Bob is patient with Stephen, but at times, his frustration for all that he is doing to support Stephen shows through. "Well, Jesus. What did I do last year?" he asks Stephen. "I drove you back and forth to school. Blew up the engine in my truck and everything else." Elaine's husband is older, age fifty-seven, and was ready to retire to play golf. As she says, "He wanted to retire in Florida, so he's a very unhappy man."

But while some are upset by life's turns, others have adjusted, like Tony.

For Tony, life changed almost overnight. Tony, age sixty-one, took in his granddaughter Amanda and her brother when their mother, who struggled with drug addiction, no longer could care for them. She was in rehab at the time of the interview.

Although he and his grandchildren are "bonded" now, it was not an easy transition for Tony. The sudden return to parenthood was very difficult, he says: "You know, like my whole life has changed back around now." He used to drink with his friends and enjoy the companionship of women. But now, he says, "I'm not drinking with buddies anymore," and he hasn't had a date in a long time. "I wouldn't even bring a woman in the house. It's not because I'm older. I don't know if it's [because] I've had time to sober up or what. And then you think back to the things you did do wrong, you know?"

He admits that the change at first was too much and he sank into a depression.

"I enjoy being alone sometimes," he says. During that first winter, he would take "every minute I can and lay down and watch TV."

To add to the initial difficulties, he and his grandson were not close. When he first arrived, Tony says, "I kept thinking, geez, he's easy to take care of and everything, but I'll be glad when he goes back home."

Tony is gruff and a little rough around the edges—he's been married several times and knows his way around a bar—but he loves his grandchildren dearly, and he wants only the best for them. Amanda, at age fifteen, is entering her teens and pushing the boundaries as far as she can, and Tony is not a fan of many of her friends, though he is trying to keep an open mind. They struggle about curfews and her desire to sleep over at her friends' homes, including with boys.

"You con me," he says to Amanda, when she calls to tell him where she is. "Then you've got to wait for a few days for the truth to come out."

"Why? Because you're old and kind of . . . dumb?" she teases.

He lets that one pass: "Well, I don't know who you're with. If I knew who you were with . . ."

Amanda replies, "No, because whenever I call you and tell you who I'm with, you start flipping out and saying, 'Oh, I don't want you with them. Get home.'"

For her part, Amanda is trying to adjust to living in a house full of men, and she is sometimes embarrassed by the situation "because you and Riley share a room, and our house stinks like a cigarette," she says.

Her grandfather also watches her boyfriends like a hawk. "I'm still a guy, and a guy is a guy no matter how old he gets," he tells her. "I know exactly what's going through that guy's head, whether he says it is or it isn't."

"But he hasn't tried anything," Amanda complains.

"Because he knows I'll hunt him down like a dog!" says Tony.

But for all his gruffness, Tony is also a softie at heart, and Amanda knows and appreciates it. Grandparents and grandchildren, she says, "have a way stronger bond than a parent and a child."

"Well," Tony adds, "it's a different kind of bond. Because you're a grandparent and a parent."

"But I think grandparents are way more trusting and reliable," she says.

Today, two years since that first winter when they arrived, Tony now knows that life without them would be hard. He wants his daughter to be successful in rehab, but he knows that would also mean the children would return to her.

"It might be a good feeling, I don't know. But then it's like you're just stuck out there in the world alone, you know what I mean? It sort of changed your whole life, and now if they're not living with me anymore, I got to go adjust back to being a regular person," says Tony.

"I Really Miss Being That Grandmother"

In addition to the challenges that come from playing an active caregiving role during a time in the life course in which it is not typically expected, grandparents raising grandchildren must negotiate a new role, no longer a typical grandparent but not the parent either. Stephen's grandmother Jeanne laments the shift to parent and away from the fun-loving, spoiling grandmother she used to be. Before he came to live with her, she and Stephen would go out to lunch or shopping together—"Come home with new sneakers and jeans," Bob, his grandfather, sitting nearby, interjects.

"Even when he was younger, it would be 'oh, I have a half day of school tomorrow, do you want to pick me up?' I said I'd love to," Jeanne says. "We were so close."

But, she continues, talking to Stephen, "I obviously can't be in that role right now. I really miss being that grandmother. I'm still your grandmother, and I always will be, but for right now, I can't possibly be a caretaker and be that same grandmother. It's like a person that's been lost that I don't have anymore."

And that, she says, "is a tremendous role-turning. He was the firstborn grandchild, and it was like—that's just not there anymore. It's almost like my daughter's role now."

Indeed, Jeanne feels that she and her daughter, Carrie, have switched roles, with Carrie now the fun adult Stephen sees on weekends and Jeanne the one who provides the day-to-day caregiving and discipline.

"It's not fair," she says.

Sherry, too, "grieves that loss, of not being able to be a grandparent to my grandchildren," though she admits to still spoiling Melissa, her granddaughter. "Sometimes I do things, and I say they're a grandma thing," she says.

Joanne, who is raising Rebecca and her two siblings, also misses her grandmother role. Her daughter is living two doors down, addicted to drugs.

"I'm going to wake up one of these times, going to find her dead in her apartment. I really am. Her damn place is condemned. No electric, no gas, no nothing," says Joanne.

Rebecca, meanwhile, is a straight-A student but is still a teenager, rolling her eyes at her grandfather's demands and making life hard for Joanne. Money is tight, and Joanne's husband is not working. Joanne is now doing it all, she feels.

And the added stress of raising three teens is too much. She misses the days when they just visited and were just her grandchildren.

"It used to be good with my grandchildren," she says. "It was good before they were living in my house. They [were] always, you know, always polite and everything else. You know, I'm just so alone. I just want my babies back—that's all I want is my babies back. I just feel like I've lost them all," she says, breaking down and crying.

Darla, on the other hand, is getting a second chance at being a "regular" grandmother again. Her oldest daughter has just graduated from nursing school and announced that she was expecting her first child: "So it's like I'll be getting that role of grandma back."

Holly recognizes that her grandmother Cathy may not want to know her, warts and all, now that they have started living together just less than a year ago. "I mean, I see you as my grandmother. I didn't want you finding out, like, certain things about me because you are my grandmother," says Holly to Cathy.

"You don't want us to see you're human," Cathy adds.

"Exactly," says Holly. "You're the people who can hype us up on sugar, send us home." But in this case, Holly is home: "That's the problem. I live with you!"

Chrystal also expresses empathy for her grandparents, saying, "You want to be like the grandparents what spoils us and actually act like grandparents and give us presents and everything. But you can't do that because you guys are stuck in this situation."

Barbara also spoils her grandchildren, as a way of hanging on to the grandmother role: "I tend to be more lenient than I was before [raising my own children]. I want to be the grandparent. I want to do the things that grandparents should do instead of being the hard person."

One grandchild, at least, acknowledges that perk. "Being raised by a grandparent is, I don't know, it's easier because your grandparents is more lenient than your parents would be sometimes," says Stacy, age eighteen. "And they're more on your side. When you need things, you know you can go to them. That's the best thing about living with your grandparent."

Stacy and her great-grandmother, Marsha, are very close, and Marsha readily agrees that she spoils her. "It's different from raising your kids," she says of raising grandchildren. "You tend to spoil them, give them more leeway than what you gave your own."

"Not the Real Parent"

The issue of whether a grandparent raising a grandchild is considered a parent or a grandparent is a complicated one. The grandparents I interviewed differed starkly on whether they referred to themselves as parents or whether they maintained their identities as grandparents and emphasized that they were not the children's "real parents." For Lucille, Lindsey's great-grandmother, it was important to retain her identity as the great-grandparent rather than the parent. This meant that she did not pursue the idea of adopting Lindsey because, for her, it would mean taking over the role of Lindsey's mom. Adopting her, she says, "would have been one of the worst mistakes I could have made because I feel like children should be with their parents."

Other grandparents feel that their actions are more highly scrutinized due to the fact that they are "not the real parent." For example, Betty describes a walking-on-eggshells feeling as she raises Adam: "If one of my kids fell down, they're my kids—they fell down. Adam may be my kid, but he's not really, is he? So, God forbid something would happen. My

God, if the parents come out, they'll come after me; I'll look like the bad guy."

Another grandmother, Estelle, felt that raising grandchildren meant she never had the final word on decisions, which was difficult.

"Raising my teenagers, to me it was easier. They were mine," she says. Her grandson, Michael, on the other hand, is a different story: "This is my daughter's son, and for me to do certain things and I got to call her and ask, 'Can I do this with Michael? Can we go here?'" Estelle had learned the hard way to always check in. When she didn't include her daughter in decisions, she "got accused of a lot of stuff that weren't true."

In some instances, grandchildren can take advantage of these feelings of caution or sympathy and refuse to listen to the person who is "not the real parent," making discipline harder. Christine, Joshua's grandmother, had a saying when she was parenting her own kids: "The rule stands." Now, however, her grandchild does not respect her authority as much. "It's kind of confusing because I feel like you're my child," she tells Joshua. "But you're not my child. You're my grandchild, so sometimes it's hard. Because if it was my kid, the rule stands."

Grandparents also have a firsthand view of the challenges their grandchildren have faced during their young lives, including abuse, neglect, parental death, and voluntary abandonment by their parents, as highlighted in chapter 1. Sometimes that means they take greater pains to see to it that life is easier for their grandchildren. Elaine says to her grandson James, "When you love someone, you want to be good and firm, but you also don't want to hurt someone that's been through a lot."

Grandparents also sometimes feel guilty for what their grandchildren have gone through and often try to make up for it by being lenient. Shirley, Christopher's grandmother, wonders sometimes whether she is to blame for her son's irresponsible behavior toward Christopher. "A part of me goes back to the old [thought]: You couldn't do a better job with your own kids, so how do you think you can do with your grandson?" she says. Indeed, a key challenge for grandparents is how to talk about the difficult circumstances that led to the formation of their grandfamily, while at the same time reassuring their grandchildren how glad they are to be raising them.

This tension is evident when Karla tried to explain to her granddaughter, Chrystal, how she came to live with them.

"You did it for our health, because you care about us," Chrystal, age fifteen, says of her grandparents' decision to take her and her brother in. "You guys didn't do it because you wanted us, did you?"

"Yes! We wanted you very badly," Karla explains.

"I thought you did it because we were, like, in bad situations or something. Like, Mom and Dad didn't really have the money to care for us and stuff," says Chrystal.

"Well, a lot of that was true. We were trying to help your parents because they couldn't financially support you two. And Grandpa and I was in a position where we could help them out by doing that. We also didn't feel that your parents were totally mature enough to take care of the two of you. But you were definitely wanted—and still are," says Karla.

In reality, Chrystal's mother had been charged with child endangerment for an abusive situation. Their father had taken them after that, but he lost his job and starting drinking, so the grandparents stepped in. Chrystal's mother would later be charged with additional counts of child endangerment with her later children.

Virtually no grandparent sets out intending to raise his or her grandchildren. In that sense, as Chrystal believed, they did not "want" to raise their grandchildren. However, all the grandparents felt extremely fortunate to have the opportunity to raise their grandchildren. Indeed, this tension between sadness for the reasons that their grandchildren came to live with them and thankfulness for the opportunity to raise their grandchildren pervades many aspects of the role grandparents play in the lives of their grandchildren.

Legal Struggles

A very large number of grandparents I interviewed described the challenges brought about by the tenuous legal relationship they have with their grandchildren. For these grandparents, there is a very real possibility that their grandchildren might go back to live with their parents at any time.

As Elaine, James's grandmother, says, "Sometimes it's hard for me because I think you're going to go: 'I'm going to go back home with Mom.' And I think to myself, 'Ho, am I ready for that if he does that?' And yeah, that's going to be very hard for me. But I mean, that's part of it. That's what a grandparent has to say."

That possibility makes it difficult to fully embrace the parental role and, as I will show in the next chapter, it makes it easier for the grandchildren to dismiss the grandparent's efforts to take on a parental role.

There are numerous types of legal relationships grandparents may have with the grandchildren they are raising, ranging from adoption (relatively rare in my study) to various forms of legal custody, either temporary or permanent. Other legal issues pertain to whether either or both of the biological parents have visitation rights, as well as whether they pay any child support to the grandparent. For the majority of grandparents in this study who have not adopted their grandchildren, issues of custody and visitation are continuously revisited through repeated court visits, which are costly both financially and emotionally. I am not a lawyer or expert in family law, and as such, a full discussion of the legal issues facing grandfamilies is not a focus of this book. In addition, chapter 5 will describe some recent policy changes that attempt to clarify legal issues within grandfamilies. However, the legal relationship between grandparents and grandchildren in grandfamilies does influence the relationships between family members, which are the key focus of this book.

The complexity related to legal issues, and how it influences family relationships, is evident in Erica's family situation. Erica's grandmother Molly has been to court several times for various custody hearings. She first fought for custody after her son Joe's marriage broke up and he was unwilling to keep Erica. He was happy to relinquish custody in exchange for not having to pay child support. Later, Erica's mother sued for custody, claiming Joe was not her father, but ultimately backed away. A few years later, Joe would seek custody again after he started living with another woman, but the judge sided with Molly, opting for a more stable situation for Erica. Eventually, Joe was given visitation rights, and Erica and her father began seeing one another more regularly. But then that too faded, and now Erica wants nothing more to do with him. Erica has rekindled her relationship with her mother and regularly visits her, even though there is no legal arrangement requiring their visits. That, too, causes strain in the family, as Erica's mother is more lenient about rules and "is more of a friend than a mother," according to Molly.

Repeated visits to court are especially painful when the "opposing" side is your own child. Grandparents may try to give their children (the grandchildren's biological parents) the benefit of the doubt, supporting visitation or other custody arrangements in the hope that the parents will turn things around. As Adam's grandmother says, "We all feel the same way, that our kids will get their act together and everything will be good again."

But sometimes, after several contentious trips to court, grandparents concede that it may be best to take the helm. Nora, fifty-eight, has been to court several times over custody of her two grandsons, Matthew and Jamie: "As far as my son, I love him dearly, but I don't necessarily like him. He has put the kids and myself in so many chaotic things. I didn't realize it until going to court the last time that I was actually contributing to the kids' emotional disturbance because I was allowing him to come in and out, in and out."

Her son is a veteran, having served in Iraq and Afghanistan. He is also a serial dater, bringing home a new woman every time he visits his sons, which upsets both boys.

Jamie is "really, really angry with his dad and he's chosen to go to—I call it the dark side—the Goth and stuff," says Nora. Matthew, on the other hand, "will say that he's really angry with his father, and he doesn't want to talk to him and this and that." But when his father calls, "It's just like his heart melts," says Nora.

The anger and conflicted feelings make it hard on Nora when she has to go to court. "Every time he got a new girlfriend, every time he got a new wife, we went to court," she says, and only much later did she realize she was entitled to a lawyer.

But each time, she explains to the children that the judges are thinking only of the children's best interests: "And like I told the kids many times, that I choose to go the court route for the fact that I'm not right always, he's [father] not right always, and the court will determine who the best placement of them are."

But the toll it has taken is apparent. "I was taken in and out of courts so many times, and it cost me so much money, and it was really, really overwhelming," she says.

Sherry, Melissa's grandmother, has learned from experience that sometimes it is best for grandparents to "right away get some kind of order of custody," as painful or scary as it may be to engage in legal battles with the parents, "because when I first had the kids, a parent could come by ten years later, when the kids were able to have jobs and help support the family or take care of other siblings. They could just come and whisk the kids out of the home, and there wasn't anything anybody could do about it."

Unfortunately, many grandparents are not in clear-cut legal situations and, in the words of Justina, Amy's grandmother, are forced to "just play it one day at a time."

"The Definition of the Word *Parent* Is Not Necessarily Biological"

While some grandparents struggle with what name to call themselves and face legal ambiguities as well, others go out of their way to describe themselves as their grandchild's parent, and they have upfront conversations about their role.

As discussed earlier, Tara came to John and his wife as a toddler, when her mother was on the verge of dropping Tara at social services owing to her drug problems. Tara has since completely severed herself from her mother, her grandfather says.

After a recent visit by her mother, John recalls, "Tara said, 'I really don't like my mother,' and when I asked her why, she gave me adult answers. We were shocked because Tara is extremely perceptive. She learned to read people at a very young age."

Tara "has her mother pegged," says John, who, as noted earlier, had just retired owing to a disability when Tara arrived. To complicate matters, Tara's mother is John's stepdaughter. The complications of what *family* or *parents* mean are often front and center with John.

As he says, "From the very beginning, I realized I had to dismiss the fact that this is a stepgrandchild. In fact, I've never even used that term with her. It's also sad because I have to be both father and grandfather, and that's why instead of calling me *Grandpa*, she calls me *Papi*, and that's a compromise."

Tara seems to take both the nontraditional family situation and her grandparents' role as her parents in stride. "Other than us," she says, only one of her classmates has parents who are still married. "The fact that she says it like that," says John, referring to the "other than us" mention, "means that she does really regard us as her parents."

"We've explained that there's a difference between the mother and father that give birth to you; they're not necessarily the same people that raise you, so that the definition of the word *parent* is not necessarily biological. She understands that, and so do we," says John.

The role of a grandparent and the words used to describe him or her (*Grandma* versus *Mommy*, for example) are important indicators of the nature of the relationship between the grandparent and the grandchild. Sometimes grandchildren in the same household use different words for *Grandma*, depending on the nature of their relationship. Charlene, who is raising five grandchildren, told me that her oldest granddaughter, Liz, whom she has raised since infancy, calls her *Mommy*. Liz refers to her biological mother (whom she sees almost daily) by her first name. In contrast, the youngest child calls his grandmother *Momma* and his mother *Mommy*, a system that he came up with on his own. The other three children call her *Grandma*. She attributes these differences to the ages at which the children arrived in her household, the order in which they arrived, and her bond with each of them.

"Yeah, that's the best thing," says Liz, nineteen, of her close relationship with Charlene. "That's why I love being with her. It's like I have a stronger bond with her than my own mother. I don't even call my mother *Mommy*." Liz was a young child when her grandmother adopted her. Liz's mother, Brittany, was in and out of rehab, and Charlene stepped in then: "I said, 'We going to court because you not going to let those people take my grandchild.'" And, she says, "I've had her ever since." Brittany has since kicked her drug habit, and she visits nearly daily, says Charlene. "But none of the kids want to go back to their mother," she says.

"She's my mother," says Liz, pointing to her grandmother, "because she's been there for me my whole life. I can't call nobody *Mommy* that wasn't there my whole life. So she's my mother."

"The other kids call me *Grandma*," says Charlene, "which I can understand, because I didn't really bond with them this way."

Warmth and Appreciation

My research team and I spent countless hours watching, rewatching, and coding the videos we made while interviewing grandparents and grandchildren talking together and the audiotapes we created while interviewing the grandparents alone. In almost all of these videos, the thing that stood out the most was the great warmth and appreciation between grandparents and grandchildren. We also felt that what we were seeing was unique. Grandparents and teenagers repeatedly and overtly expressed their feelings of love and appreciation for each other in ways that we felt were not common in other family types.

Grandparents talk about what the love they get from their grandchildren means to them. Laura says of her grandchildren, "Those are my prize packages," while Elaine says to James, her grandson, "I guess we are just very specially blessed to have this kind of relationship."

One reason for such a high level of warmth is likely related to the fact that our sample of grandparents has *chosen* to raise their grandchildren. These grandparents went out of their ways, often against very challenging odds, to bring their grandchildren into their homes and lives. In this way, grandparents raising grandchildren are those who demonstrate the greatest love and commitment to their grandchildren.

It is also possible that the unique situation in which grandparents and teenaged grandchildren find themselves leads them to develop a greater sense of appreciation for each other. In expressing their love for each other, both grandparents and grandchildren often refer to how their love for each other is greater than their love for others in their families.

Perhaps it is not surprising that both grandparents and grandchildren, each of whom have been hurt in some way by the parental generation, would feel that their relationship has particular benefits and meaning, especially in contrast to their relationships with the parents. What is remarkable, though, is how many grandparents and grandchildren in my study took a very difficult situation—the hurtful actions of the parents—and used it to build and reflect upon a very positive relationship with each other.

"Keeps Me Young"

One of the benefits of raising a grandchild that is mentioned by numerous grandparents is that their role as a grandparent caregiver provides them with companionship, pushes them to try new things, gives them someone to look after, keeps them active, and generally keeps them young. As Shirley tells her grandson Christopher, "I get to do things and have someone to do them with. It keeps me active and doing things that I enjoy doing and that I wouldn't have the opportunity to do if you weren't here."

Grandparents raising grandchildren enter a world of after-school activities, school engagements, summer camps, and sporting events. While these activities can be exhausting, being part of them also creates a sense of energy as well as numerous opportunities to interact with younger adults and other children, all of which can help grandparents stay young and active.

Ashley's grandmother Nancy says that the best thing about living with Ashley is that it helps "to keep us young."

"I keep her up-to-date in the fashion," Ashley adds. At least, she says, "I try."

"You keep me up-to-date on the computer stuff, right?" says Nancy.

Betty, too, appreciates the way Adam challenges her way of thinking, forcing her to expand her mind-set.

"I admire your intelligence," she says to Adam. "You start talking about things that are over my head because you're good in science and math, which has not been my thing. When we start talking about the stuff, you're so knowledge-able. When you start to say some things, it's just great. . . . I enjoy that. I don't know about you, but I like it a lot."

"I know you laugh at me because I come out with all this stuff," she continues. "But we were told thirty or forty years ago that this is the way it was."

Adam, she says, keeps her updated. "[I] like updating your data," he adds.

She and Adam also travel, which Betty enjoys. "I'm looking forward to our next trip," she tells him. "I think overall we have a good thing going."

Christine and her husband are also spurred to travel more with their two grandsons, Joshua and Jake. "We take the kids camping" far and wide, she says. "I mean, just jump in the truck after school and take them—go wherever we want to go. Adventure."

Her husband is also active with the boys, Christine adds: "My husband is a fisherman, so he'll take the boys. He takes them swimming. We also do historical things with the kids too. You know, you get out, walk around."

As shown in table I.2, more than half of the grandparents interviewed were not married. For grandparents living alone, and whose children have left home, the presence of a child in the household is very welcome. Indeed, grandchildren themselves recognize the ways in which they keep their grandparents young, active, and engaged. As Alex, sixteen, says to his grandmother Sinead, sixty-eight, "You're always on the go. You're not just sitting there, watching TV all the time, doing crossword puzzles."

Added Support

As noted previously, a high percentage of the grandparents in this study had health problems. For these grandparents, the presence of their grandchildren in their homes provides not only companionship and purpose but also assistance in addressing daily health needs.

"I've had some medical difficulties, and she's taken care of me," Janice, age sixty-four, says of her granddaughter Sarah. "She's a good child. I don't know if I would have really made it if it wasn't for Sarah."

"You're crying," Sarah says, startled, jumping up to get her grandmother a tissue.

"I'm not going to cry," Janice says, laughing. "I would do it over again. She's a wonderful child, and she's been a great help to me."

In the interview, the two were clearly close, gently teasing each other and laughing in an easygoing bond. Her grandmother's health was a worry to Sarah, though she said nothing to her grandmother at the time.

"Sometimes," Sarah says during their dialogue, "when you get sick, it interferes a lot. But that rarely happens anymore. You're doing a lot better."

"Was it hard on you?" Janice asks.

"A little. Just a little. A tiny bit. But I got through it because I had friends who I talked to a lot," replies Sarah.

"You took care of me for . . . oh, I guess, two months at least, wasn't it?" asks Janice.

"It felt like years. It felt like years going by," says Sarah.

"She never complained, never said anything," Janice says to us later.

Do-Overs: Being a Better Parent the Second Time Around

For many grandparents, the role that they play in the lives of their grandchildren can't be described without focusing on an appreciation of having a "second chance" at parenting. This second time around, they can apply what they've learned over the years, which often means a more open and understanding relationship.

Andrea's grandmother Monica is grateful for her second chance to "get it right" with Andrea. "My second chance twenty years later," she says. "I was really surprised but also happy . . . oh, I was in heaven." One of twelve siblings herself, she had always wanted to have more children, but she was unable to have more than one, her son, Jamal.

When she was raising Jamal, she worked two jobs "so we didn't have to go on welfare," and she wasn't always around to monitor her son's friends.

"The people that he chose to be his friends were much older, doing different things, things I didn't see," she says. Her son is currently serving a sentence in prison.

But with Andrea, she is trying to offer more guidance, even when Andrea objects.

"Because," she says, "I cannot let her fail. I told her, 'There's so many kids who don't have moms and don't have dads, and they raise up above their adversities, and that's what I want you to do.'"

Numerous grandparents reported being more relaxed when parenting for the second time. Part of this had to do with having gone through the experience of raising kids and, perhaps, coming to the somewhat humbling realization that there is only so much that caregivers can do to influence how a person turns out. Patty came to realize that things she thought were important, such as keeping a clean room, aren't as crucial in the big picture.

"I pick different battles now," she says. "If Lila doesn't clean her room, it's not as important now as it was when [my daughter] was home. Having your room cleaned . . . doesn't make you a good person or a bad person. Those are things you just learn through experience."

Similarly, Jeanne talks about how her reaction to Stephen's new haircut contrasts to how she would have reacted if her own child had done something similar years ago: "As a parent now, I don't take things as personally, and I don't take it so much as a reflection of myself. Stephen just got this Mohawk haircut, and I was like, 'I can't believe this,' but

I didn't say it that way to him. Whereas when I think back to when my own kids were sixteen, if they came in with a haircut like that, I would be like a lunatic."

For others, this greater relaxation had to do with the fact that their grandchildren were simply easier to raise than their children, many of whom had multiple emotional or behavioral problems, even during childhood. Others note that the world is more accepting of children with behavioral issues, when in the past, parents often blamed themselves.

Sue, whose own daughter, now forty-two, had serious behavioral issues as a child, says, "She was having all the acting-out problems and everything, and so there was a lot of guilt the first time around." Back then, she continues, "they didn't even acknowledge that kids could have mental illnesses, you know, let alone have resources to treat them." Her daughter's behavior was "bizarre," Sue says. "No one put a name to it, and consequently, we spent a lot of our time feeling as though our parenting skills weren't enough to satisfy her needs, you know? You feel like you're just not adequate to the job."

Other grandparents report being stricter this time around, having learned from what they perceive to be past mistakes. As Karla, Chrystal's grandmother, says, "I don't think my grandchildren get away with as much as my children did, because they taught us all the things to watch out for." Similarly, Monica is "overprotective" of her granddaughter Andrea in order to keep her out of trouble.

Another strength grandfamilies revealed is their sense of being better prepared to be parents than when they were raising their own children. This was often attributed to the greater wisdom, self-knowledge, and experience that come with age.

Several grandparents talked about learning from past mistakes in parenting. For some grandparents, raising their grandchildren is a second chance to make amends. As Stan, Chad's grandfather, describes it, "I get a second chance. When we were raising kids, I didn't get to see them that much, and I was working, and when I wasn't working, I drank a lot. There's some bad years for me, and I really didn't know what was going on with me at that time. Now I have the opportunity to try it again, and I'm enjoying it a lot more."

Others have reformed their parenting styles. Numerous grandparents noted that they no longer spank the children they are raising. "Times have changed," they say. Others are more relaxed parents. Still others talk about the benefits of living in a time with a greater understanding of the behavioral and emotional issues children may face and appropriate parenting practices.

Grandparents also talked about the greater maturity that comes with age and how it helps them to be better parents the second time around. "I personally find I have more time for Lila," says Patty. "I'm not busy chasing my tail finding out who I am. So I have more time to play with her. And I know a little bit more about what's important about raising a child and what's not, what matters."

Several grandparents mentioned that the fact that they are not working gives them more time to spend and enjoy with their grandchildren, compared to when they were balancing work and raising their own children. Finally, other grandparents also mentioned the value of simply having had experience with raising a child. Laura says, "When I was raising my kids, I was learning how to be a parent. Now with my grandchildren, I give my grandchildren love I couldn't give my kids."

Another common theme among grandparents is the rewarding feeling that comes from raising someone from early childhood to the verge of adulthood. As described earlier, most of the grandchildren in this study had been living in a grandfamily for a very long time. Because of this, their grandparents had the opportunity to see them grow from toddlerhood into burgeoning young adulthood.

As noted previously, Tara has been with her grandparents since she was a toddler, twelve years now. For John, her grandfather, it means that he has had the chance to experience the joy of "seeing a twenty-six-month-old toddler growing up to be a fine young lady." Part of that satisfaction comes from his sense that he has both protected her and steered her toward a good path.

"We realized that as long as we had Tara, we had an obligation to protect her," he says of himself and his second wife, "and one of the first things was to protect her legally. So we went to court within a couple of days [after she was left by her mother] to get custody of Tara."

John also wants to protect Tara physically and emotionally, even if that means keeping her away from her mother and especially from her father, whom they believe may have sexually molested her.

"I don't know if I could exercise self-control if I knew who her father was. I think I might know who the father is, but maybe it's better that I don't."

Tara's mother, he says, is too irresponsible to care for her. "I keep myself focused on the fact that my responsibility is not the mother, because the mother is an adult. My responsibility is the child and to keep this child safe," he says.

John also takes pride in his role in Tara's success. He has played a role in that success, in part because, this time around, he is a more patient parent and understands Tara perhaps better than he does his own children. He raised twin girls and a son, all of whom are in their forties now.

"I have a lot more experience than I had," he says of his parenting role. "That part is very good because I understand her. I understand some of the things that she does and why."

Tara has attention-deficit disorder, which John also experienced as a child. "I was hyperactive, and I guess they just didn't have a name for it. My mother used to say, 'I hope one day you have a child like this,'" he says, laughing. "So I understand some of the things that she does and her inquisitiveness. I help to steer her in the right direction so that it works for her."

Tara seems to agree. Though they have their typical parent-child spats, when asked the best thing about living with grandparents, she says, "It's rewarding because you can learn things." Parents in their thirties, she says, don't have as much time for their kids and are not as mature: "They don't know anything because usually they're young and they're not smart."

She also understands her unique position. "Not that many people in the world are raised by their grandparents," she says. "I don't know the percentage, but it's not a lot. It's a once-in-a-lifetime [situation]."

Tara, John says, is blossoming before his eyes. He sees it when Tara speaks to their church group on Wednesdays during workshops. "Tara has been giving presentations. She can lecture with the quality of an adult on a subject, when she's prepared," he says proudly. "I don't think that adults give children enough respect, and you can't expect children to respect adults if they haven't been taught by example."

Like John, for many grandparents, a source of pride in their role is the feeling of rescuing grandchildren from difficult or unsafe situations and ensuring that they are being raised "the right way." For grandparents who often had to sit on the sidelines while their children struggled in raising the grandchildren who eventually came to live with them, being able to take control of the situation is welcome. As noted by Abby, sixty-seven, who is raising her granddaughter Leah, age fifteen, "I know where you are. I know you've been well taken care of, and I know you're not being abused by anyone. I thank God that I have my health and strength and I'm able to provide for you guys and raise you the way that I want you to be raised."

"We're Just Very Specially Blessed to Have This Kind of Relationship"

Several grandparents discussed the special bond that forms when they tap into the best of both roles: parent and grandparent. For some grandparents, the special bond between them and their grandchildren is a direct line to each grandparent's own child, particularly if that child has died. Ashley's grandmother Nancy says, "I think the best thing is that I still have part of my son in Ashley," and Lisa, who is raising her grandson Patrick, age fifteen, says, "I get to actually see the reincarnation of my children" in her grandchildren. "Like my granddaughter, she's the spitting image of her father. She acts like him; she puts that little silly grin on her face like him." Her grandson, she says, looks just like her other son.

Other grandparents report that the bond with their grandchildren is stronger than the one they had with their children. "I love my kids," says Ingrid, sixty-eight, of her son and his siblings, "but with Whitney, it's like a true love. She's my granddaughter, and she's my daughter."

Janice and Nancy share a similar bond. As described earlier, Janice leaned on Sarah, her granddaughter, when Janice's health wavered, and Janice is extremely grateful, tearing up while telling the story during the interview. But Janice has also been there for Sarah. Sarah was born with heroin in her system. Sarah's father was a drug dealer, and "he got my daughter into drugs," Janice says. "He started her with marijuana, and finally, it went from marijuana to cocaine to heroin."

Janice confronted him about his role in her daughter's addiction, but he claimed to love her. Janice's daughter would later die from an overdose.

Janice got custody of Sarah that day at the hospital when they discovered the drugs in her system. Sarah has been with Janice ever since. It has been eighteen years since Sarah has seen her father.

"I think the last time her father saw her was [when] she was probably maybe three months old," at a custody hearing, says Janice. "He didn't touch her or anything. He just, you know, walked by us and saw her." He had threatened Janice with violence, she says, so she fled the state with Sarah at the suggestion of the local child protective services.

"I asked her if she wants to get in touch with her biological father, and she said no," Janice says.

Janice and Sarah have a very close bond, which is apparent in the easygoing and joyful way they converse with one another in interviews.

"I'm close with my children," says Janice, "but Sarah and I have this certain bond. I can't describe. And I never felt that much of a bond with my own children. I don't know, there's just something, we just click together. And I think being older . . . being older I was ready for more of a responsibility, you know, and like I said, she was a baby, and I just loved her to death."

"I find it to be a wonderful experience," Janice continues. "I would do it over again. And the best thing is how well she's turned out to be. She's the best thing that's come into my life. I raised her brother and her sister, who are out on their own, but she's the best."

"I know I'm the best!" Sarah chimes in, laughing.

"You know you're the best!" Janice laughs. "And I love her to death. What do you have to say?" she asks, turning to Sarah.

"I agree with you. I'm the best child in the world!" They both laugh.

"Technically," Sarah adds, "to me, you're more like my mom than my grandparent."

"Right. She's always said that, since she was little. She would always tell me that. She's a joy to heaven in my life," Janice says, tearing up again.

"Crybaby," Sarah whispers, smiling.

"Oh, yeah." They both laugh. "She keeps me smiling. She keeps me young and happy."

"I'm not sure about the young part," Sarah teases.

Later in the conversation, when asked what was tough about being raised by a grandparent, Sarah had no answer: "I can't really name anything because every day is a good day."

Other grandchildren also recognize the special bond that comes with the dual role of grandparent and parent. "If a grandparent and a grandchild live together," says Tony's granddaughter, Amanda, age fifteen, "they have a way stronger bond than a parent and a child."

The Role of Religion

A final key strength of the grandfamilies I interviewed is religion. Both grandparents and grandchildren reported that religion was a very important part of their lives, and they relied on their beliefs to give them the strength to take on the challenges in their lives.

The vast majority of the families I interviewed (fifty-six out of fifty-nine) were Christian, with the most common denominations being Catholic (22 percent) and Baptist (19 percent). In all, 89 percent of grandparents described themselves as "very" or "fairly" religious, as did 65 percent of teenaged grandchildren. A total of 85 percent of grandparents reported praying every day, and 40 percent said they attended services at least once per week. When asked about the role of religion in their lives, the most common responses among grandparents were that it provided them with peace and strength.

As Susanna says, "I'm just waiting and hoping and praying that one day I will be able to see God for myself and let Him say, 'Well done . . . because I know you had a hard time.'"

Susanna and her children had lived "in the projects" for eleven years when Jordan, her grandson, was younger. Jordan is happy that she is in better straits now, she says, because "like when we was in the projects, when you come on the elevator, you don't know who was on the elevator with you. You don't know who's coming upstairs, who's going down. But now, you've got a decent place to stay."

"Right," says Susanna. "I thank God for being there. Because before I got there, I prayed and asked the Lord to take me out of the projects because I was tired. I was tired of it. And He did."

Susanna and others also use the church as guidance for their grandchildren. Susanna is trying to get Jordan back to church because she feels it is where he learns the discipline needed to stay off the street.

"He been in church ever since he was a baby," she says. "That's how I started him." But since his older brother has stopped attending, "so he figure, well . . . I can stop. I want him to stay there because when he's there, it keep him from doing bad things."

She tells Jordan, "You've got to listen. When you go to church, don't just go there. Go and listen. And take heed. And do what the preachers preach. Do the right thing. Not the wrong thing. When you've been taught the right thing, you do the right thing. Because a whole lot of children out here, they're not taught the right thing. They don't go to church. Their mothers don't take them. They don't know. So you can't hold them responsible for something they don't know. But you can hold you responsible, because you've been going all your life."

Laura, too, uses the church as a source of comfort. Her two granddaughters were born addicted to drugs. But she says, "I don't look at that was a hardship. I look at it, and I said, 'Lord, I thank you for bringing my kids, and I love my granddaughters.'" Similarly, Ray's grandmother Aurora sees God as having a hand in her life: "There was a reason why I only had one child, because God knew that I was going to have all the rest of my daughter's children at one point of time." Perhaps Monica captures it best, saying to Andrea, "God answers prayers, and He allowed you to come into my life just when I needed you."

Conclusion

As this chapter makes clear, several factors make it challenging for grandparents raising grandchildren to clearly define their role. Ambiguity over who is really the parent, lack of clarity on the legal relationship, and the difficulties in taking on a parenting role in an untypical part of the life cycle all present challenges. These challenges center on the fact that the role of a grandparent in a grandfamily household is often undefined, changing, and surrounded by ambivalent feelings regarding how and why the living situation came to be in the first place.

At the same time, virtually every single grandparent I interviewed felt that the joy and benefits that they derive from their role as caregiver vastly outweigh these challenges in defining their role. These benefits range from direct care and companionship provided by their grandchildren to an increased sense of purpose and engagement in the outside world that being a caregiver brings. Some grandparents find raising their grandchildren to be an opportunity to redeem themselves from what they see as past mistakes or simply an opportunity to raise children again as an older and wiser person with more experience. Others simply appreciate the chance to be a parent again, something any empty nester can likely appreciate and that grandparents realize is a unique situation not many others have.

In the next chapter, you will hear from the youths about how they perceive their roles as grandchildren being raised by grandparents. As I hope this chapter shows, the grand-families I interviewed inspired me with their numerous strengths. Despite challenges of financial hardship, legal battles, health problems, and difficult relations with the parental generation, grandparents and grandchildren expressed love, appreciation, and warmth toward each other. They repeat-edly discussed how grateful they felt to be living together in what they saw as a uniquely special living situation. In this way, grandfamilies can remind all of us of the value of appreciating those with whom we have the opportunity to live and love.

3

"I Get All the Love I Need"

*How Do Youths Define Their
Roles in Grandfamilies?*

Being a teenager can be hard, but teenagers in grandfamilies face particular challenges. Research in psychology tells us that two central tasks of adolescence are to define one's identity and to create a meaningful narrative about one's family and life. These are tall orders for any youth, but those living in grandfamilies face unique obstacles in achieving these goals.

Despite this, most of the teenagers I interviewed tackled these challenges head on. Many expressed hurt or confusion about the fact that they were not living with their parents. However, most youths also expressed exceptional maturity and warmth as they considered their roles and relationships to those around them, finding value in the opportunity to develop a unique and special relationship with their grandparents. In this chapter, I discuss how youths define their roles within grandfamilies. I start with a discussion of adolescent identity development in general, focusing in particular on the role that families play in fostering this development. I next discuss particular challenges that teenagers in grandfamilies may face in this process. Then I describe the varying ways that teenagers in my study saw their roles within their grandfamilies.

The Challenge of Adolescence

The reason adolescence can be so challenging is that teenagers are taking on very hard work—forming their own identities as unique individuals with core beliefs, clear relationships with others, and defined roles in society. Teenagers challenge the viewpoints of parents and those around them as they seek to define their own beliefs, try on various roles to see what fits best, and seek increased privacy as they develop independent relationships with peers and others. The famed psychologist Erik Erikson recognized how difficult these tasks are, describing adolescence as a period of identity crisis. According to Erikson and others, it is essential to work through this crisis in order to emerge as a successful adult who has a sense of self and the role she can play in the world.[1]

During this identity-formation task, teenagers begin constructing their life narratives. Prior to adolescence, children lack the cognitive skills to be able to reflect critically on their lives and the roles of others in them.[2] During the teenage years, youths begin to be able to think carefully about their own lives, their histories, and how they relate to others. Research emphasizes how important life narratives are, serving as stories that go beyond just the simple facts of a person's life and instead involve active construction on the part of the individual in order to create a story that makes sense and is meaningful. In creating life stories, research tells us, people describe their pasts, understand their current situations, and prepare for their futures.[3] Such life stories are distinct from memories but rather have a "plot" and "characters" just like any other story. Researchers emphasize that life stories are essential for creating unity and purpose in one's life. While people begin putting together their internal life stories in adolescence, these stories continually evolve over time as they incorporate new knowledge and experiences into their lives and narratives. A key component of a life story is that it is coherent—it explains how the different events in one's life relate to each other, giving meaning to one's life and experiences. Rather than just a random assortment of events ("first I did *this*, then *this* happened, and then I did *this*"), one's life begins to take shape as something that is more coherent and unified ("I'm the kind of person who does *this* when faced with situations like *this*").

The identity-formation process of adolescence is not only hard work for the youths themselves, but it can be challenging for caregivers, as teenagers often seek to establish their own identities and beliefs by rejecting those of the important adults in their lives.[4] Indeed, parents and caregivers often find this process more stressful than teenagers do. However, families play a key role in teenagers' identity-formation processes, and a central challenge for family members is to keep a strong connection with their youths while at the same time allowing the identity-formation process to evolve. Research shows that families can foster teenagers' identity work by being warm but firm (displaying what is often called "authoritative parenting") and giving their teens the autonomy to develop their own opinions and beliefs and to disagree with their caregivers while still communicating with them and holding fast to nonnegotiable rules and values. Indeed, the family has been referred to as an important "training ground" in which teenagers can have a safe space to try out various identities and beliefs.[5]

When working out one's identity, it is important to incorporate not just facts and positive events but also difficult and complex events, such as death, divorce, or problematic interpersonal relationships, into a coherent narrative. Often these difficult and challenging events are ones that have occurred in the teenager's family. All families face challenging events; the key is for families to be able to discuss such events or dynamics in an open way so that youths can think critically about them and develop their own beliefs about how such events play into their own narratives.[6] For grandfamilies, this is particularly important.

Betty describes this process and its challenges well, saying of Adam, "When he was little, you'd see him smile more in pictures. You never see him smile now. As he got older and became a teenager, you know, the hormones are flying anyway, and then he starts thinking about 'Gee, these two [his parents] are really lousy.' So when he got to be a teenager, you know, then it started to get bad with him."

Karla, for example, tries to draw out Chrystal to talk about her feelings toward her parents. Karla feels that Chrystal's conflicted feelings are the source of their communication issues and regularly tries to get her granddaughter to open up more about her parents. But Chrystal is reluctant. Sitting together during our interview, she asks Chrystal, "What makes you hold your feelings so close to yourself and not share them?"

"I don't know. Because I don't want to talk about them," Chrystal answers.

"What is it about it that you don't want to talk about them?" asks Karla.

Chrystal replies, "Because it's, like, when I talk about stuff that makes me feel, like, hurt or something, and then I just feel even worse after talking about it, because I have to think about it. I'd rather just, like, shove it back and don't think about it, and I'm good."

"Do you understand that when you keep shoving it back and shoving it back and shoving it back, that it comes out in actions that Grandpa and I don't always understand why you're behaving the way you're behaving? Where if we knew what you were thinking and all that garbage that you're hanging onto in your brain, that we could help," says Karla.

"It's not that easy to just go and express your feelings," Chrystal says. "For me, anyway."

When conflict between family members and complex events are unresolved or not discussed openly, the identity-formation process is made more difficult and prolonged, creating challenges in developing the skills and sense of self needed in adulthood. Similarly, when there is confusion about one's role within a family, the identity-formation process is more difficult.[7]

As this discussion makes clear, the identity-formation process is a profound and challenging time for all youths. Teens being raised by their grandparents may face particular challenges: they live in a unique family formation that few or none of their peers may experience, making it difficult to identify models of how youths are supposed to behave in such families and also potentially creating a sense of being different or strange. Youths being raised by their grandparents may also not be sure what roles they should play with their grandparents (are they grandchildren or children?) and with their parents (whom should they consider the "real" parents?). In addition, the reasons youths came to live with their grandparents in the first place are often complex as well as unpleasant. Because of this, the youths themselves, as well as their family members, may, like Chrystal, have a hard time discussing those key events, even though doing so is essential to the formation of a coherent narrative and healthy family functioning.

To my knowledge, no other study has examined the identity-formation process among youths being raised by grandparents. However, research on youths who are adopted can shed light on what youths in grandfamilies may go through. Such research tells us that as adopted children grow up, some can develop more questions, and more nuanced questions, about their birth parents and how the circumstances of their births and adoptions relate to their current lives.[8] Taking on the typical adolescent role of challenging parental rules and beliefs, adopted teens may begin to idealize what it would be like to be raised by their biological parents, leading to difficulties in their relationships with their adoptive parents to whom they compare this idealized relationship unfavorably. They also may begin to examine their own characteristics and tendencies, wondering which aspects of themselves derive from their birthparents. This is normal given the central task of adolescence, which is to answer the question "Who am I?"[9] Adoptive parents have a key role to play in managing these explorations and feelings by being open and communicative with their adopted children. Evidence suggests that this type of questioning period is an expected, even healthy, stage of adolescent development for adopted youths and that most make it through such a stage with stronger senses of self and connection to their families.[10]

This research suggests that, similarly, grandparents in grandfamilies have an important role to play in walking their grandchildren through the sometimes tumultuous, but ultimately crucial, identity-formation processes of adolescence. Importantly, despite the challenges of not only being a teenager but being a teenager raised by a grandparent, the main emotion that came through when I talked to youths about their roles in their families was one of warmth and appreciation. Next, I discuss what youths had to say about their families, starting with that most important aspect: warmth.

She Has Been There My Whole Life

The youths I interviewed recognize the unique situation they are in and appreciate the benefits that come with living in a grandfamily. Over and over again, my research team and I were struck by the frank and touching sentiments of love, warmth, and appreciation expressed by the teenagers we interviewed. While we have no direct comparison, we all felt that we were seeing something unique and special. These feelings of love, warmth, and appreciation stand out as a noteworthy strength of many grandfamilies.

Teenagers' open statements of love and affection likely arise from several factors. First is that, like their grandparents, youths know that they are in a unique situation. This gives them an opportunity to step back and evaluate their family lives, something that teenagers being raised by parents may not typically have reason to do. In doing so, they identify many positive aspects of their lives, especially compared to what life might be like if they remained with their parents. Indeed, the youths I interviewed have a clear understanding of what the alternative to living with their grandparents would be. As they weigh their current living situation against other options, many youths feel strongly that they are better off than they would be otherwise, and they express great appreciation for their grandparents for providing them with that better situation. Grandchildren like Leah recognize that, if it weren't for their grandparents, they might be in in the clearly less desirable alternative of foster care.

Leah's grandmother Abby was working as an aide in their local hospital when Leah was born. One day, toward the end of her shift, Abby got a call. "Go down to neonatal," her colleague said, "your daughter just had a baby." Confused because her daughter was not living anywhere nearby, Abby took the elevator to the neonatal unit, only to realize that it was her daughter-in-law who had given birth to her granddaughter.

"My son got killed before Leah was born," Abby says, "so I didn't know anything about it." Her daughter-in-law had left the baby in the unit. "Got up and walked out of the hospital," Abby says. "Fighting for her life, and she left her."

Abby took over and raised Leah with no further input from her daughter-in-law. There is little talk of either of her parents today. Now, at age fifteen, Leah has a grounded sense of her situation. She wants the things most teens want—to hang out with her friends, go shopping, and have the latest fashions.

She shrugs when her grandmother reminds her that she doesn't need designer clothes, so long as she's clean and looks neat. "I got bored wearing the same stuff over and over and over and over," she says of her wardrobe. Although Leah is a typical teen in that respect, she also stands out from her friends because of her sensitivity to her and her grandmother's unique situation.

While Leah may chafe at her grandmother's rules and views, she also realizes that they are not made of money and her grandmother is doing the best she can. While she would love to have a new wardrobe when she starts high school next month, she knows she also needs "boots on my feet" when it gets cold. "I need a job!" she suddenly announces.

She also knows that all of these "wants" are a privilege because she could have easily ended up in the foster care system.

"At least you're being raised," she says of her situation, "and not just, like, somewhere where you don't know nobody and you're getting sent from foster home to foster home and going to this random house that you've never seen before."

At least, she continues, "you're not walking around feeling like nobody cares about you or you don't know if you've got a family out there."

On Abby's part, at age sixty-seven, it isn't always easy caring for a teenager, but she says, some things never change. "The years are different, but the parenting, the nurturing of the children, is still the same," she says.

One thing that has changed, however, is life on the street. "When your children are out there on the streets, with friends, you're wondering if they're going to get caught up in a cross fire or something or gang related or something," Abby says.

Their neighborhood can be a struggle, especially for Leah, who on the precipice of high school has become aware that life is precarious.

"The hardest thing is just basically growing up and how, like, everybody getting locked up or like everybody's dying." There are few places she can go, she says, "without seeing the people that you've got problems with."

A trip to Africa was a good wake-up call for Leah, though, Abby thinks. Leah came away from that trip with the realization that, despite the troubles in her neighborhood, she is one of the lucky ones.

"You just got a chance to see how other parents, grandparents raising grandchildren, live," Abby tells Leah.

"And," Leah adds, "to let you know there's more people on this planet that's less fortunate than you. And they don't have as much as you have."

"You have a lot to be grateful for," Abby says, and Leah nods in agreement.

Even more common was for youths to explicitly compare what it is like being raised by their grandparents to what it would be like if they were still living with their parents. Adam puts it bluntly, saying to Betty, "I don't really know about the best thing, but maybe it's just having somebody there for me when my actual mother wasn't." Jordan takes a more emotional approach, telling his great-grandmother, "Without you, God only knows where I would be. And I'm just thanking you for that." Similarly, Amanda says to her grandfather Tony, "I can trust you way better than I can my own parents, because you've always been there for me. You've never did anything wrong to me. I think grandparents are way more trusting and reliable [than parents]."

For some youths, thinking about what it is like to be raised by a grandparent raises very difficult thoughts about the role their parents play in their lives.

When asked what the best thing is about living with a grandparent, Andrea begins to answer but then starts to cry.

"The best thing is just knowing that somebody loves me enough to raise me," she says.

"Don't cry, sweetie," her grandmother Monica says, taking her hand.

"If it wasn't for you, I probably wouldn't be here because my mom didn't want me," Andrea continues.

As noted in chapter 1, Andrea's mother had abandoned Andrea as a toddler on the pretense of attending college. Monica's son, Andrea's father, Jamal, was in prison at the time and remains there. Andrea's mother would later remarry and have more children.

Monica reassures Andrea, saying, "Of course I love you! Where do you think you're going to be? You're my life. Don't you know that?"

Andrea nods, wiping her eyes.

"You would be nowhere else," says Monica.

Sometimes the things that youths appreciate about living with their grandparents tug on your heartstrings because they are so basic. Megan, age fourteen, appreciates that "I know I'm in a good home without anything illegal. I'm living in a good, clean home." Marcus, nineteen, says, "Being raised by a grandparent is better than being raised by your mother. Grandparents are nice to you." Sean, thirteen, says simply, "I got a roof over our head, and I'm not poor."

Some teenagers even appreciate that their grandparents have rules, which they believe their parents would not. Victoria, age seventeen, says, "If I stayed with my mother, I'd be getting in trouble every day because she doesn't have rules." She adds, "Sometimes your parents don't give you such good advice." Courtney, age fifteen, appreciates that her grandparents push her to get an education, saying, "They push you and get on your nerves to the point where you just want to start screaming and yelling. But it's for your own better."

Grandparents are not only better than their own parents when it comes to raising them, say some of the teenagers I interviewed, but also better than the average parent, due to factors such as maturity, having more time, and having more love than parents. Tara tells her grandfather that parents usually work and don't have as much time to spend with their kids compared to grandparents. She also appreciates the maturity that grandparents have, saying, "People that are in their thirties, they don't know anything because usually they're young and they're not smart. I don't think they know much." Similarly, Lila appreciates that she benefits from her grandparents' greater maturity and life experiences: "I feel like I do a lot more things than my friends might do, living with their parents, because you guys have gone so many places that my friends' parents haven't."

The importance of maintaining a family bond, even though they are not living with their parents, is highlighted by several teenagers. Some recognize that they get to have a special relationship with their grandparents that most children don't have. Ashley appreciates that by living with her grandparents, she remains within the family circle, saying, "I still have pieces of my father [who is deceased] with me." Ashley goes on to say that she really likes it that she also shares a physical resemblance with her grandmother and that people would think they were mother and daughter, joking that now that her grandmother has gone gray, though, that happens less often. Similarly, Jason, age fourteen, whose mother's boyfriend was abusive to him and wanted Jason to leave after Jason's mother became pregnant with the boyfriend's twin babies, says that he appreciates that he remains in touch with the rest of his family, as well as being able to "have an adult figure in my life that is part of my family."

Finally, several youths mentioned that a key benefit of being raised by a grandparent is being spoiled. Although April and her grandmother Mona fight frequently, often about April's mother, April can sometimes play that to her advantage. Mona knows the pain April has been through and wants to make up for it as much as she can. When her grandmother notes that they sometimes disagree about April's love for brand-name clothes, April says, "Not really, I get my way."

"No, not all of the time," her grandmother replies.

"Most of the time," April answers.

Similarly, Christopher says that the best thing about being raised by a grandparent is "getting what you want, when you want it." Lila notes that by living with her grandparents, she is "more spoiled" than her half-sister, who lives with her parents, saying, "It's fun."

"I Have to Count on You Instead of My Mom and Dad"

As mentioned previously, the overwhelming majority of youths' discussions of what it is like to live in a grandfamily involved statements of love, appreciation, and affection. Although much more rare, it is still important to note that not all youths expressed these sentiments. Some youths mentioned being embarrassed by the fact that they live with their grandparents. Matthew says, "You don't have your mother or father with you, and so kids at school don't really understand," and Alicia, age twelve, says it is hard that her grandmother, not her parents, comes to her school and sporting events. Seeing her grandmother in the audience amid all the other parents simply reminds her of what is missing.

For other youths, the pain involved in the fact that they don't live with their "real parents" overshadows feelings of warmth or appreciation they might have. These youths have very ambivalent feelings about being raised by their grandparents, which, as illustrated in chapter 4, can also hinder the grandparent–grandchild relationship.

Trudy sought custody of her son Scott's children, Alicia and her brother, when Alicia was seven and her brother was twelve. Their mother had been deemed unfit by a judge after letting her son miss nearly a year of school, and their father had skipped town. Trudy stepped in because "that's no way for kids to live." Trudy has few warm feelings for her son or Julie, his wife, whom she believes were never cut out to be parents. Julie had an older child that her own mother had raised, and Julie lived with her parents on and off for years. She had met Scott, and they'd had two children, but the relationship did not last.

"Personally," says Trudy of her daughter-in-law, "I think if she couldn't have the man, she didn't want the kids. That's the way I saw it. She just didn't want to be bothered with the kids. Neither one of them needed to be parents, let's put it that way."

Julie has largely since disappeared from their lives, seeing them maybe once or twice a year, even though she still lives in the area.

Trudy is at times disgusted by the turn of events and worries that the children are irreparably harmed. Alicia's brother is in therapy, and she'd like Alicia to join. But Alicia resists. "This wasn't how my own kids was raised, because their father didn't walk out on them, and I was their mother, and I didn't walk out on them, so they didn't have that hurt," Trudy says. Alicia has begun rebelling and has become sullen lately. Trudy is bewildered by the about-face that Alicia has taken, even if she understands where it springs from. Overnight, it seems, she's gone from a happy-go-lucky girl whom everyone "adored," Trudy says, to a stranger.

"Kids always want their mother's love," Trudy says, which is one reason she gives Alicia, just now entering her teen years, more room. "I realize she's like this because she's—she's hurt. I know she's angry about it, but I don't think she know how to express it. She's just mean sometimes." For Alicia, her parents' absence is deeply felt. In school, she's often embarrassed by the fact that she lives with a grandparent when teachers ask for a parent's signature or need parents' input.

"I see everyone else with their parents," she says, "and I have my grandma there. It's hard. It would be cool if, like, if my parents would help you out and stuff, but they don't. The hardest thing in being raised by a grandparent is that sometimes you don't get to see your parents a lot, and you kind of miss your parents and stuff."

That tension is apparent in the interviews, where Alicia answers in monosyllables as Trudy desperately tries to draw her out and reassure her that it will get better.

"I think if me and you could sit down and talk about things," Trudy tells her, "I think we could get along a lot better with a lot less stress."

"Mm-hmm," replies Alicia.

"Because we used to have a lot of fun and stuff."

"Mm-hmm."

Trudy adds, "And I do wish we could really talk about a lot of things easier and more quieter and not so stressful."

Alicia nods. Later, Trudy takes another approach, reminding Alicia that she needs to step up and become more responsible, but again gets no response.

"You still have to buckle up and do things because you have to grow up and take care of yourself. Grandma don't know how long her health is going to be good in here," says Trudy.

"Mm-hmm."

Trying again, Trudy says, "You don't get what you want from your parents. And sometimes you get angry."

"Mm-hmm."

Trudy continues, "I don't like walking around and not being able to talk to you and stuff like that. If I say something, you get so upset. And sometimes I just figure, well, it's not really worth it."

"Mm-hmm," Alicia replies again.

"You know? Because all you're going to do is get upset. And I can't get you to understand where I'm coming from. But I figure if we pay more attention to each other's feelings . . . do you agree?"

"Mm-hmm."

"Because you know we used to be real close to each other really."

"Mm-hmm."

Trudy says, "I want to go back to stuff like that. Like we sit around and talk about the fun that we all had when we used to get together and have cookouts and stuff."

"Mm-hmm."

The interview ends with nothing resolved, an example of the ways in which anger toward the entire living situation can spill over to the grandparent–grandchild relationship.

Matthew, too, is angry. As noted previously, Matthew's father is in the military and a serial dater, bringing a new woman home every time he visits, which is less and less frequent. Matthew still clings to the hope that his father will be the stand-up guy he wants him to be, and each time they talk on the phone, Matthew's "heart melts," his grandmother says.

He's struggling with his situation more now. When asked what it's like living with grandparents, he says, "It's like a banana split without the banana. You don't have your parent. You don't have your mother or father with you, and so kids at school don't really understand as much. They kind of see it differently."

Lately he wants to emulate his father and enroll in the military, but his grandmother wants him to focus on school and go to college. They fight often.

"I'd rather you just sign me papers so I can work, so I can get some money," Matthew says.

"No, I will not do that," answers Nora.

"I know, I know, I know," he says emphatically.

The two begin to needle each other.

"And you haven't showed me where you've changed any, Matthew," says Nora.

"Nope!" Matthew replies.

"Not even your attitude, right?" asks Nora.

"Nope."

"And why is that, Matthew?"

"Because I'm tired of doing chores for free," he says.

"Really?" retorts Nora.

"Yeah," Matthew answers back.

"Well, if you're tired of doing chores for free, then what do you think I feel like?" Nora asks finally.

"I don't know," Matthew says.

They continue to argue over Matthew's chores, especially his inability to keep his clothes off the floor in his bedroom. But to Matthew, Nora is too hypercritical and doesn't trust him to do it right.

Nora says, "Matthew, when I give you the trust and I ask you if you're doing it—"

"You don't give me trust," he interrupts.

"Yes, I do," says Nora adamantly.

"There's no trust," Matthew insists.

Her frustration and exasperation are clear by now. "It's a never-ending job," she says of raising him. "And the more that I do, the less you guys appreciate. Everything has changed."

Again, this conversation remains unresolved, an underlying tension that Nora attributes to Matthew's anger toward his parents.

Grandparents Are Stuck in Their Time

Several youths mention the generation gap between themselves and their grandparents as something that hinders the grandparent–grandchild relationship. Chelsea, eighteen, complains that grandparents are "stuck in their time." "Grandparents confuse this for the sixties!" she says.

Chelsea, in her last year of high school, chafes at her grandmother Nina's overprotectiveness, which she sees as a direct effect of her grandmother's age. Chelsea feels like she's an adult and needs to experience things for herself and that her grandmother just doesn't understand. Nina agrees it's good to experience things, but she just wants to protect her from experiencing bad things with lasting repercussions.

"The grandparent feels that she wants to protect you from things," Nina, sixty-seven, tells Chelsea.

"No," Chelsea interjects, "grandparents want it their way."

That way, Chelsea thinks, is far too out of touch. Chelsea is staying out late this last summer before college, and Nina worries about her. She's afraid that Chelsea is walking home alone late at night.

"God forbid, with all these things going crazy in the streets, shooting around the area, and all these things," Nina says. "You should not be walking alone. You should be walking with somebody."

"You can't walk around in a plastic bubble," Chelsea tells her grandmother. "If you're not naive and you know how to handle yourself, you don't get into trouble," she claims.

They finally settle on a compromise that Chelsea will be careful, though it is a begrudging one from Chelsea, who still believes she knows more about life as a teen than her grandmother ever could.

Alison, age fifteen, puts it more harshly, saying that the hardest thing about being raised by her grandparents is "dealing with old people constantly." Her grandmother is fifty-two. Similarly, Stephanie jokingly says to her grandmother Barbara, age fifty-five, "We are in the twenty-first century! You are so set on your time period and that era. There's better music [now]. No offense to you, but I do not like the music that you came from. And better clothing and definitely better dancing." Chad, thirteen, also jokes, saying of his grandfather, age sixty-three, "He grew up in a tooooootally different time. I mean he grew up in the BC era."

Chelsea isn't alone in her frustration with her grandmother's overprotectiveness and her own desire to cut free of the bonds. Edie and her granddaughter, Brittany, argue about Brittany's friends. Brittany wants to "hang out" with her friends at their houses, but Edie is leery.

"If they come down to our neighborhood," she says, it would be fine with her. But "I don't want you going down to their neighborhood. You know I've got to see you 24–7," Edie says.

"That's annoying," Brittany says, rolling her eyes.

Emily's grandmother Michelle, fifty-six, worries about Emily's exposure to movies and television shows in what to her is a bewildering era of *Naked and Afraid* and violent movies. Asking Emily, who was sixteen at the time, what kind of movies she watches, Emily shoots back: "Ma, we have basic cable. I can't watch anything bad."

"I'm just trying to cover you," Michelle explains. "When you get to get big, you can do whatever, but not now."

"Watching something bad on TV isn't going to affect me," Emily says.

"Oh, yes it is," replies Michelle.

"How, Ma, how? How? How? How?" asks Emily, her voice rising.

"It puts things in your head," Michelle says, "things that aren't supposed to be in there, in the head of young kids."

"Ma, there's plenty of stuff in my head, and you don't see me shooting anybody," says Emily.

As any parent of a teen will recognize, there is the inevitable argument about parents "just not understanding." And of course, there are the arguments about dating as teens stretch for more autonomy and push back at the old-fashioned boundaries their older grandparents have, in their eyes, unnecessarily imposed. Andrea and her grandmother Monica get into a heated exchange about boyfriends and her grandmother's old-fashioned protectiveness.

"I don't understand why I can't date," Andrea says, "and I don't understand why I have to tell you every single boy I talk to."

Monica explains that she needs to learn to trust Andrea more, and Andrea's recent behavior has not helped: "When you say you're 'hanging out,' and I find out that you're somewhere where you're not supposed to be, then you're going to be in trouble."

"So that's why I can't have a boyfriend?" Andrea asks.

"No. You can't have a boyfriend because you're twelve years old. You're not mature enough to have a boyfriend," replies Monica.

"You don't know how mature I am. You just don't want me to grow up," says Andrea.

"It's not true," says Monica. "I want you to grow up. But I just think that right now your responsibility is to your education."

"This is stupid. I'm going to be mad with you until I'm allowed to have a boyfriend and I'm allowed to see who I want to be seeing," says Andrea.

While most children get frustrated at some point about their parents being out of date, the larger gap between grandparents and grandchildren can be a "double whammy," says Christopher. Because of their age, grandparents are out of touch with both other parents raising teens and the teens themselves. Amanda, Tony's granddaughter, puts it clearly, saying to Tony, who was sixty-five at the time of the interview, "You don't know what life is like nowadays because when you were growing up it was a long time ago. You don't understand my perspective of things because you're not as young as I am or as a regular parent would be." Emily, age sixteen, echoes that sentiment, saying of her fifty-six-year-old grandmother, "Because they're older, grandparents don't get you. Parents don't get you either, but with grandparents it's even harder because they're even older, and they insist on giving their view[s] on everything, even though what they're talking about happened like a hundred years ago."

Lucille, great-grandmother of Lindsey, states the perspective of the older generation: "We can see farther than you. We see danger. And sometimes you all really can't see it. So this is why we try to gear you in the right direction, so you won't have to face this danger. But there are times you all don't feel like we know what we're talking about."

Lindsey beseechingly expresses her feeling that Lucille doesn't understand what life is like for teenagers today, saying, "It's a new generation . . . times is completely different. . . . You're not, like, in the midst of what is really happening, like, what's really, really happening with the generations. Y'all say, 'This is how it is because we know,' . . . but then it's like, 'Do you really?' You might say that you see farther, but honestly, we're living in it, so we have to learn every minute from experience." Lindsey tells Lucille that she, Lindsey, is actually living life "firsthand," while Lucille is just "home watching the news" to get a sense of what is really going on in the world.

Erica and Molly are having similar struggles, though this time about premarital sex. Erica's mother, who has recently come back into her life, is much more lenient about boys, letting Erica's boyfriend sleep over when Erica visits. "She's old enough to do what she wants," Erica's mother claims. But Molly worries that Erica will get in over her head or, worse, become pregnant.

"Well, you have to make up your own mind," Molly tells Erica, about whether to have sex with her boyfriend or not. "Hopefully you won't have to pay the consequences, because, you know, if you look at your mom and your dad. You won't be happy."

"I definitely would, like, take precautions," Erica tells Molly, reassuring her that she knows what she's doing. "I've taken, like, years of health classes." Plus, she says, "I have real-life situations that go with it. It's not like most people, who really don't have that family experience like I do."

"Yeah, because the person that pays the consequences is always the child," Molly reminds her.

"I know," Erica responds, with the worldliness of a budding teen. "I'm, like, one of them, so I know." More so, she says, than girls who "just let it happen."

"You know," Molly adds, trying to explain her and her husband's rules, "we try to understand that. And we want you to date. We'd like for you to do those things. But we want you to make the right choices, and sometimes we can see things that you don't see. Because we are older."

"I know," says Erica, "but you have to make your own mistakes in life. You have to learn from mistakes."

"Right, but we don't want the mistakes to be too costly," Molly says.

"I know," replies Erica.

Communicating with any teen about dating and similar topics can be challenging, but especially so under the unique circumstances that grandfamilies face. These include issues mentioned in previous chapters, such as the crossover role that the grandparent plays as both parent and grandparent, the grandparent's role in instigating their unique living situation, and as shown here, communicating across a large generation gap. Combined with these issues are the daily stressors grandfamilies face, including financial strain, legal wrangling, and health problems on the part of both grandparent and grandchild.

As Stephanie and her grandmother Barbara reveal, life as a teen is hard, and life as a grandparent of a teen is uniquely hard.

Barbara says, "Oh, the hardest thing is, you know—"

"Me being a teenager?" interjects Stephanie.

"Yeah," says Barbara, "just realizing that you're getting older and starting to have a life, a little bit of a life, and I'm being too protective."

"Yeah. A bit," says Stephanie.

"And you talking back is a little bit hard for me too," says Barbara.

"I'm sorry," Stephanie says, "but you just kind of annoy me so badly. I feel like I'm so entwined with you, your life. Like, everything I do has to be, somehow be, related to you. Like, that's the thing. I can't listen to music, like the music I want to listen to, when I'm around you."

"You've just got to communicate more with me," Barbara responds.

"I try to, but then you get so upset at me because I say something, and you're just, like, 'AAAAUGH!' You go into a rampage. It's funny watching you," Stephanie says.

"We both need to sit and listen to each other," Barbara adds, "and not get upset with each other."

"Just chillax and listen," Stephanie says.

"Yeah," agrees Barbara.

One area where the generation gap is particularly striking has to do with teenagers' use of technology. Numerous grandparents expressed frustration that they could not understand or keep up with the ever-changing technology used by their grandchildren. Most were aware that technology both is here to stay and has the potential to be dangerous and that they should have a good understanding of what their teenagers are doing, but many are unable to do this. For example, Jennifer complains that her grandmother Patrice asks "the retardedest questions" about computers.

"I wasn't trained in the computers, so I really don't know," Patrice replies. "That's why I'm asking you, because you're a smart cookie! And you know, you should have a little bit more patience with an older person."

Likewise, Laura, age thirteen, tries to convince her grandmother Sandra, seventy-four, to get her a web cam.

"I don't see why I'm not allowed to have web cameras," she whines. "I mean, everyone else has web cameras."

"I don't understand what a web camera is," Sandra responds, "for one thing."

Sandra worries that a teenager could get in trouble with a web camera, asking, "Do you take pictures with a web cam? Or is it just for communicating?"

It is "just for communicating," Laura replies, though she dodges the issue of whether pictures can be sent to others using a web cam.

"I'll have to ask your aunt and uncle who know more about this than I do," Sandra says, ending the conversation.

Betty, sixty-three, mentions Adam's time on the computer as a key issue of disagreement between them. "I try to understand that you enjoy it. But I also think, 'My God.' Hour after hour. You just never come up for air," she tells him.

"You have no clue what I do in there," Adam says proudly of his time on the computer in his room.

"No, I don't," Betty concedes.

The result of his extended time in front of the screen, she says, is that they rarely communicate anymore. By the time he is done playing, Betty is long in bed.

"I can't call you an addict. But you get on it as soon as you get home from school," Betty says.

"Not true," Adam says.

"Oh, you get something to eat first," admits Betty.

Betty tries suggesting that he get off the computer by 11:00 PM each night: "I mean, really, because you need to go to bed. There's no reason why you can't adjust it so you can go off at eleven o'clock."

"I have insomnia, OK?" Adam replies. "I'd hardly be tired."

"Oh, God, Adam. You have to," says Betty.

Adam says, "I'll say I'll try, but we both know that will just be—"

"Well, by ten o'clock, you start to wind down," interrupts Betty.

"OK," he finally agrees.

"Oh, OK. Well, we'll work on it. I don't know how much we resolved that problem," she adds, having been through this before.

Knowing They Won't Be There Forever

Finally, some youths express a fear that their grandparents will die while still raising them. When asked what the hardest part is, Erin, Paula's granddaughter, says, "Seeing your grandparents being sick."

Paula has a serious heart condition and was finding it hard to breathe because of water retention, which left her laid up on the couch.

"I was pretty sick there for a while," she concedes. But with a new prescription for fluid retention, she feels much better. "Look how skinny I got—I mean that was all water on me. On my lungs and on my chest. On my legs. It's, you know, hard getting around when you don't feel good. That's hard for you," she says to Erin. "But we all know that there's God—"

"And He can heal?" Erin asks.

"And He can heal us if we pray. So don't worry about me being sick. I'm going to be here. OK? That's what bothers me more than anything in the world, is you kids worrying about that."

Erin nods, trying to be brave: "I don't want to worry, but it's hard."

In a later interview, Paula says, "Erin worries about me . . . because she knew how sick I was. I want her to know that it's OK. I've made provisions for everything."

For children who have already lost their parents either to death or abandonment, the fear of losing another caregiver is particularly strong. Stacy, as described earlier, has a very close relationship with her great-grandmother, Marsha. When given a choice, Stacy chose to stay with Marsha instead of moving in with her mother, LaToya (Marsha's granddaughter). Stacy says poignantly, "The hardest thing is knowing that they won't be there forever, and then you'll have to go on your own and can't lean on them no more. You have to grow up."

Conclusion

Something that all teenagers and their families must go through is the tumultuous, exciting, and crucial process of forming one's own identity and developing a narrative of one's life. For all teenagers, this process is helped when the caring adults in a youth's life are open, communicative, understanding, and allow for and answer the numerous questions about self and others that emerge during this time.

The challenges of adolescence can be greater for those living in grandfamilies. Such youths are in a unique living situation that may leave them feeling different and isolated from their peers. When forming their own life stories, they may begin to question long-standing situations and relationships for the first time, such as why they came to live with their grandparents in the first place, what role their parents play in their lives, and how they relate to both their parents and their grandparents. A larger-than-usual generation gap, and anger and confusion about the role of the parent, can make this process even more challenging and can negatively influence the grandparent–grandchild relationship.

Fortunately, for the vast majority of grandfamilies I interviewed, these struggles and questions are taking place among a backdrop of warmth, love, and appreciation. We saw in the previous chapter the strong feeling of love that grandparents have toward the grandchildren they are raising and the many benefits they feel they receive by raising them. In this chapter, we see that this applies to the teenagers as well. The youths that were interviewed were remarkably candid about the warm feelings they have toward their grandparents, looking their grandparents warmly in their eyes and telling them how much they are appreciated. This strong undercurrent of love and warmth provides an excellent and safe space for teenagers in grandfamilies to tackle tough issues head on and emerge on the other side with greater wisdom.

In many ways, those living in grandfamilies serve as role models for the rest of us, reminding us to appreciate the unique bonds that we have, even if they are not perfect.

4

"I Love My Daughter, but I Don't Like Her Right about Now"

The Role of Parents in Grandfamilies

Despite living outside the household, parents can play a central role in the lives of teenagers and grandparents in grandfamilies. As described in chapter 1, many children come to live with their grandparents due to an informal arrangement in which the parents voluntarily give up the child. Most children's parents are not deceased or incarcerated, and many still live nearby. Because of this, nonresident parents are able to play some role in their children's lives, and many do. This chapter describes the various types of relationships youths in grandfamilies have with their nonresident parents.

It is important to note that this chapter on the role of parents in the lives of grandfamilies is limited by the fact that I was not able to interview any of the absent parents themselves. Therefore, what is presented here are the perspectives of the grandparent and grandchild regarding their relationships with the absent parent. I surely would have been able to tell a more nuanced and richer story had I been able to interview the parents. However, doing so is challenged by the fact that grandparents can be hesitant to involve the absent parents in their lives, by the mental health and substance abuse issues that some absent parents have, and by hesitations that absent parents likely have in talking about why their children are not living with them. Given how important these parents can be in children's lives, though, I am currently undertaking a new study that is designed to hear from the absent parents themselves. In the meantime, however, when reading the stories presented here, it is important to keep in mind that the perspectives of the parents themselves are missing.

For some youths, the relationship with the absent parent goes smoothly. Lila, age fifteen, is an extremely outgoing and social girl. When she was little, her grandmother Patty once brought her home a few Barbie dolls and put them on the couch: "I said, 'Look who came to play.' And she starts to cry and said, 'I wanted real kids, Grandma.' I think she always wished there was more people living home."

Today, Lila has numerous friends and stays very active, whether riding horses, bowling with friends, attending summer camp, or playing numerous sports in high school.

"She has so many activities, I say to her now that you're getting older, a lot of them overlap so you have to make choices," says Patty, aged fifty-four. "And she says, 'I want to do it all.'"

Lila came to her grandmother's home when she was an infant. Her own mother, Nina, was only fifteen when she had Lila and was uninterested in keeping her. Nina, says Patty, was a handful as a teen, always sneaking out of the house, skipping school, and doing drugs. But as the years have passed, Nina has stayed in touch with both her mother and her daughter Lila. Each weekend, the three go shopping together, and Lila visits her mother frequently.

"Mommy is the older sister," Patty says. "Lila likes to go over and hang out with Momma. Her and Mommy, they do things on the computer together, and Mommy will download songs for her because Grandma don't know how to do that."

Lila can also turn to her mother for the kinds of questions that girlfriends discuss, because she sees her mother in more of a friend or older sibling role, Patty says. And, she reports, Nina would agree about her role in Lila's life.

"Nina is the first one to say, we're more like sisters than mother and daughter," says Patty.

Lila's father, in contrast, is persona non grata. Where once he was more of a presence in her life, he has slowly faded away. Two years prior, he had visited for more than a month over the Christmas holiday. The next year, he just sent gifts at Christmas. He later sent money, but, says Lila's grandmother, "after she called to thank him, he never called her back. If he doesn't come for her birthday," she says, "she's done."

Lila has come to view her father as someone who can pay for things, but "don't ask for any moral support because there's none there." As noted in the introduction, when Lila gets married, she is going to ask her grandfather, not her father, to give her away.

"I can't make her anymore call [her father]," says Patty. "She says, 'I'm tired of being a bigger person. He's the adult, he should call me.'"

As this chapter shows, Lila's positive and well-defined relationship with her mother, Nina, is not shared by all. For others, a relationship with the absent parents, while often desired, can be a source of stress for both grandparents and grandchildren alike. This chapter explores the nuanced relationships both grandparents and grandchildren report having with the absent parents.

Characteristics of Absent Parents

Very little information is available regarding the characteristics of the absent parents of children living in grandfamilies. My colleague Natasha Pilkauskas and I analyzed data on this question from the only source we are aware of, the Fragile Families and Child Well-Being Study.[1] This information, presented in table 4.1, allows us to compare three groups of caregivers: grandparents raising their grandchildren, mothers of children who are being raised by grandparents, and mothers raising their own children. All are based on a sample of relatively disadvantaged urban children.

In Fragile Families study, 41 percent of children being raised by grandparents lived within two miles of their mother, and 75 percent lived within thirty miles. Not surprisingly, given this close proximity, 75 percent of children in that study had seen their nonresident parent in the past month, with 16 percent of children seeing their mother, and 12 percent seeing their father, every day. Additionally, over half of the mothers of Fragile Families children being raised by grandparents have other children whom they are raising. These patterns are evident as well in the study presented in this book, where 63 percent of teenagers being raised by their grandparents had seen their mother, and 35 percent had seen their father, in the past year and, as noted elsewhere, it was not uncommon for parents to have other children with other partners.

In general, table 4.1 shows that grandparents raising grandchildren are more advantaged than those grandchildren's mothers. They are more likely to be married, are more highly educated, are less likely to be unemployed, and have lower rates of poverty and financial hardship. Grandparents raising their grandchildren have characteristics that are quite similar to mothers in the Fragile Families sample who

TABLE 4.1. Comparing the characteristics of grandparents, nonresident mothers, and other mothers and fathers

	GRANDPARENTS IN GRANDFAMILIES (1)	MOTHERS OF CHILDREN IN GRANDFAMILIES (2)	RESIDENTIAL MOTHERS (3)	T-TEST*
	% or mean	% or mean	% or mean	
Nonmarital birth		0.89	0.76	c
Relationship status				
Married	0.36	0.17	0.38	a, c
Cohabiting	0.08	0.19	0.22	b
Single	0.56	0.59	0.39	b, c
Age at focal child's birth M	46.50 (7.62)	21.68 (4.83)	25.12 (5.99)	a, b, c,
Education				
Less than high school	0.25	0.55	0.32	a, c
High school	0.31	0.26	0.32	
Some college	0.29	0.19	0.25	
College+	0.16	0.00	0.11	a, c

(continued)

TABLE 4.1. (continued)

	GRANDPARENTS IN GRANDFAMILIES	MOTHERS OF CHILDREN IN GRANDFAMILIES	RESIDENTIAL MOTHERS	T-TEST*
	(1)	(2)	(3)	
Labor force participation				
Employed	0.45	0.36	0.64	b, c
Unemployed	0.17	0.34	0.16	a, c
Out of labor force	0.10	0.30	0.20	a, b
Retired	0.18			
Disabled	0.12			
Health problem that limits work		0.26	0.12	c
Health status, 5 = excellent M	3.22 (1.02)	3.06 (1.26)	3.55 (1.04)	b, c
Depressed	0.11	0.17	0.12	
Substance abuse interferes with life		0.09	0.01	c
Poor	0.42	0.62	0.37	a, c
Hardship	0.40	0.66	0.50	a, c
Foreign born	0.17	0.02	0.15	a, c

Race/ethnicity		
Non-Hispanic black	0.57	0.50
Hispanic	0.19	0.26
Non-Hispanic white	0.23	0.20
Other	0.00	0.03
Own children living with them	0.56	1.00 c

SOURCE: Natasha Pilkauskas and Rachel Dunifon, "Understanding Grandfamilies: Characteristics of Grandparents, Nonresident Parents, and Children," *Journal of Marriage and Family* 78 (2016): 623–633.

NOTE: Standard deviations in parentheses.

1 Only asked about mothers (n = 54) who have had contact with the grandparent.

2 N = 32 for the mothers with children in grandfamilies because children are living with maternal grandparents.

* Denotes statistically significant differences from t-tests (p < 0.05): a = grandparent vs. mothers with children in grandfamilies, b = grandparent vs. all mothers, c = mothers with children in grandfamilies vs. all mothers.

are raising their own children, with the exceptions of age and health. Finally, the results in table 4.1 show that absent mothers whose children are being raised by grandparents are much more disadvantaged in terms of marital status, age, education, health, and substance abuse than mothers who are raising their own children. This suggests that, compared to living with their own mothers, children being raised by their grandparents are better off in a variety of ways, particularly in terms of living with someone with more financial and emotional stability.

Parents' Portraits

Chapter 1 describes how parental decisions and situations lead grandchildren to come live with their grandparents. In this chapter, I provide some profiles that describe the various parental behaviors reported by the grandparents and grandchildren I interviewed. Adam's situation illustrates a scenario in which parents' addiction problems lead to children moving in with their grandparents. As Betty tells it, when Adam was only a few days old, her son Lance, his father, pulled her aside and told her that he couldn't handle having a baby. A few months later, with Adam's father incarcerated for drug-related issues, his mother began leaving him with Betty more and more often, disappearing for days at a time with no notice. Finally, the mother also went to jail due to drugs. Betty went to court and successfully obtained custody of Adam, convincing the judge that she could provide a better home for Adam than either of his parents. When Adam's father comes out of jail, which he does often, he cycles back into Adam's life, but his continued drug addiction makes these interactions painful and sometimes violent.

Fifteen-year-old Erica's parents voluntarily gave her to her grandmother Molly when she was a preschooler, an example of a situation in which parents simply choose not to raise their children, despite living nearby and raising their other children. According to Molly, Erica's parents initially asked Molly and her husband to take Erica in. They then fought for custody of her, but when shared custody was granted, they exhibited very little interest in actually spending time with Erica. Erica's father has moved on to marry another woman, who does not approve of him spending time with her, so he chooses not to. Erica's mother, too, has remarried and has another child with whom she lives. According to Molly, the mother only reaches out to Erica when she wants to "play mom." Both parents live nearby.

Of course, not all parental involvement is negative. Estelle is a fifty-three-year-old African American woman, raising her grandson Michael, aged fourteen. She describes how she and Michael's mother, Mara, went through some challenging times but have come out on the other end with a relationship that seems to work well for all involved. Michael's mother left him with Estelle when he was about five years old. At that time, Estelle still had teenaged daughters of her own living at home, and she describes this period as a very challenging time for their family. Estelle and her daughters took turns taking care of Michael and as a result developed a great deal of resentment toward his mother, who had left town, leaving them with Michael. A few years before our interview, however, Mara had moved back to town and lives just a few houses down from Estelle and Michael and, according to Estelle, has worked hard to repair her relationship with Michael, Estelle, and the rest of the family. Estelle credits this turnaround to the fact that she never turned her back on Mara and her focus on calling everyone together for family meetings when disagreements arise. Estelle gives Mara a lot of credit, too, for being willing to take on the hard work of rebuilding a relationship with her family. Now Michael sees his mother almost every day, spends several weekends with her, and the entire family goes on vacations together.

Relationships with Absent Parents

These portraits provide some examples of the ways in which parents' lives interweave with those of grandfamilies. To provide a more systematic look, my colleagues Kimberly Kopko, Lindsay Chase-Lansdale, Laurie Wakschlag, and I analyzed the transcripts gathered from the video dialogues and the open-ended interviews of the grandfamilies I spoke with.[2] Reading through the transcripts of the forty-four youths who had some type of ongoing contact with at least one parent, we identified five themes describing the types of relationships youths have with their absent parents, according to the grandchild and grandparent reports: friendlike, ambivalent, cynical, longing, and angry. These are not mutually exclusive categories but rather broad descriptions of the ways in which we observed youths to be engaging with their nonresident parents.

FRIENDLIKE

Teens like Lila, whose story opened this chapter, have pleasant interactions with their parents but know that, unlike typical parents, theirs can't be relied on for stability and guidance. In Lila's case, she turns to her grandmother for consistency and warmth. In this way, her mother and grandmother have clear and distinct roles to play in her life. Her grandmother takes on the role of parent and her mother that of friend or sibling.

Sometimes, however, "friendlike" relationships with the nonresident parent can make things difficult for grandparents, as it does for Molly and Erica. Molly, age sixty-four, has been raising Erica, the sixteen-year-old daughter of her son, since Erica was a toddler.

Erica was three when her parents, Joe and Teresa, moved briefly away from New York in a last-ditch effort to save their relationship. But it would prove to be their downfall. Joe was drinking too much, and Teresa fell for a member of a gang. After several months of constant fighting, Teresa called Molly, warning her that if she didn't come and get Joe, she'd have him killed "and we'd never find his body." Given her gang affiliations, Molly and her husband took the threat seriously.

"So my husband got in the car and drove down there to get her [Erica], and when he did get there, my son was smart enough to say, 'I'm not going without my daughter,'" says Molly.

Thus began a long and difficult custody battle for Erica, as described by Molly. Erica's mother at one point claimed Erica was not Joe's daughter. Then Joe fought his parents for custody, but the judge was dubious. The judge said that "if we didn't settle on something, my son was not going to be happy with the decision he made," says Molly. In the end, Joe told his mother, "As long as I don't have to pay any child support, then you can have her."

After several years of distance and only sporadic contact, Erica and her mother have rekindled their relationship. Her mother remarried and had a child, and she and her new family recently moved back to New York, ten minutes from Erica's home.

Their relationship, however, is more that of friends than a mother and child, and her grandmother worries that the visits are not healthy for Erica: "Her mom treats it more like 'oh, when I want to play mom, I'll call Erica and be nice to Erica.'"

She also lets Erica have more leeway than Molly does or would like.

"Her mom tells her to do things that she knows we don't allow," and Erica is taking full advantage of that, says her grandmother.

The latest conflicts have been over boys. As described in the previous chapter, Erica's new boyfriend was sneaking into her bedroom at night when Erica was at her mom's house, and her mother did not seem to mind. Molly and her husband are trying to get on the same page with Erica's mother about what to do. But Erica's mother sees nothing wrong with the behavior. "She's old enough to do what she wants," she told them.

Molly says, "I've heard her say to Erica, 'Oh, you don't have to listen to them.'"

Meanwhile, similar to Lila, Erica's relationship with her father had deteriorated. After giving up custody, Joe still had visitation rights, though his track record was spotty. The first weekend he was to pick up Erica, he called Molly and said he had no money for the trip down from Massachusetts, where he was living with a new girlfriend.

"He moved to Massachusetts and wanted to take Erica, and my husband and I said no, you're not moving from one spot to another. This week, it's this girl. Next week, it's somebody else. She needs a stable environment," says Molly.

That relationship would also eventually end, and Joe moved back to New York, where he met and married another woman. Erica began to see her father more then, given that he was living nearby. Her grandparents were hoping her father's marriage would lead to good things for Erica, that she'd "have a dad and a stepmom." But "the stepmom did not like Erica too much" because, Molly says, "Erica reminded her of her husband's ex-wife." For Erica it was the last straw. "Erica wants nothing to do with him," says her grandmother.

For a teenager like Erica, who is chafing against what she considers to be Molly's old-fashioned rules about dating, the fact that her mother offers a more lenient alternative provides an opportunity to get away with things that she otherwise could not. Unlike the situation with Lila, Erica does not have clearly defined expectations for what roles her mother and grandmother should play in her life. She is able to take advantage of that ambiguity in ways that could potentially have long-term consequences, and Molly feels relatively powerless to stop the situation.

AMBIVALENT

Some youths vacillate between longing for their nonresident parents and anger toward them, expressing a desire to see their parents but then refusing to interact with them once they are together. Nora, age fifty-eight, describes the ambivalent feelings that Matthew, her sixteen-year-old grandson, has toward his father. Matthew's father is in the military and comes in and out of their lives when he is off duty; he brings a new wife or girlfriend with him each visit, leaving Matthew hurt that he never comes by himself just to spend time with them.

"Matthew is very angry with him and doesn't want to talk to him, but when [the father] calls, it's just like his heart melts," Nora says.

Likewise for Amy, age fifteen. One year ago, Amy's mother's boyfriend raped her older sister. The girls were immediately removed from the house, the mother was charged with neglect, and the boyfriend was convicted and sent to jail. Amy's father petitioned for custody, but the judge did not grant it. Instead, the judge asked if Justina, his sixty-five-year-old mother, would take the girls. She agreed, and the girls have lived with her for the past year.

If not for her, Justina says, "I honestly don't know where the girls would have ended up."

Both of Amy's parents live nearby, and Amy sees her father regularly, and her mother has supervised visits every weekend. Amy gets along "great" with her father and his wife, according to Justina, and she wants to be with her mother, but she's conflicted. When asked what was the hardest thing about living with her grandmother, Amy says, "Not being able to hang out with, like, our cousins and Mommy." Yet when her mother comes to visit, she ignores her.

"She interacts with me [during those visits] more than she does with her mother, and yet she wants to be with her mother," her grandmother says.

In situations such as these, with their ambiguous feelings toward the absent parents, the teens haven't settled on a clear parental role. They may not long for them, as James (featured later in the chapter) does, but they haven't totally written off their parents, as Adam has, as I will show next.

CYNICAL

Adam, a good-looking fifteen-year-old, has a very cynical view of his parents' limitations—warranted in his case. According to his grandmother Betty, Adam can tell a person every fish that ever died in his care. "He always feels it's a deep loss to him," his grandmother says.

Adam feels these losses so deeply, she thinks, because as a young boy, he kept losing his parents, first to abandonment, then to drugs.

Betty, age sixty-three, has been raising him since he was a toddler. Her custody of him has not always been without contention, and she herself is conflicted about the role her son has played in the drama that is her grandson's life. For his part, though, Adam "has moved on." Though moving on from his childhood is likely not going to be quite that easy.

Adam was only ten days old, but Betty had a sense that "something wasn't right" with her son and daughter-in-law. It was Christmas, and so she took some time off work and drove through a snowstorm to her son Lance's place.

"I brought them some Christmas presents and then just observed what was going on," says Betty.

It wasn't long before Lance took her aside. "I can't do this," he told her. Betty recalls, "He said, 'I can't, I can't be here. I have to leave.'"

Betty tried to talk him off the new-father ledge, but she could tell he was shaken. She would find out only later that he had tried to force a miscarriage by pushing his wife down the stairs in her eighth month of pregnancy. It would be the beginning of a long and fractured relationship with his son.

Months later, her son would be arrested, and Adam and his mother returned to New York to live with Betty in her small one-bedroom apartment.

Adam's mother was not prepared for parenthood. She would disappear for long stretches, leaving Betty to hustle to find a sitter, worried that she would lose her job if she took too much time off from work. "I'm trying to figure out what we're going to do, I mean, while my son's in jail," recalls Betty.

The final straw was when Adam was inadvertently overdosed with prescribed medication because of his mother's mix-up. She had given him double doses. "I was so mad, and so I went right to family court and got a custody order," Betty says.

The custody dispute was fraught. Adam's father chose to contest it from jail. But the judge agreed with Betty. In the interim, Adam would experience another great loss. A few years earlier, Betty had reconnected with John, a long-time friend, and they were planning to marry. John was keen on being able to raise Adam. John's own parents had abandoned him, and he knew what Adam was going through and wanted give him the love and stability he himself had lacked. But it was not to be. Just seven weeks before Betty and John were to marry, John died suddenly.

Betty was crushed. Adam would have "had this wonderful guy as his father, [he] would have been so terrific for him, and he died seven weeks before the wedding. So now we both were devastated by that," she says.

About this time, Lance was released from prison, and he once again raised the custody battle. "But I said, 'No, you're not going to step in here five years later. If you going to take your son, you have to work into it,'" says Betty.

The judge again agreed with Betty, granting Lance limited visitation. "I don't think any of us take this on thinking that 'all right, I'm going to have to do this the rest of my life.' We all feel the same way—that our kids will get their act together and everything will be good again," says Betty.

But for Adam, neither of his parents would get their act together anytime soon. In fact, things would get worse before they got better.

Lance arrived at their house one day several years ago, agitated and angry. He'd been out of prison for some time by now, moving in and out of rehab. He and Adam had started to develop "a little bit of a relationship," Betty says. But this day, Lance was acting very aggressively. He had been kicked out of rehab and was using again, according to his mother. He wanted to talk to Adam, but Adam was afraid of him, having never seen him in this state.

Tensions rose, and Lance attacked Betty's other adult son, stabbing him four times, before going after Adam.

"Blood everywhere," Betty says, recalling that day.

The day would haunt Adam for years, Betty says, and it would be the beginning of the end of his hope that one day, he and his parents would be a family again.

"Adam was very trusting, he believed his father really cared a lot, and he had him totally buffaloed," says Betty. "Adam is so depressed about it. He's felt this all through the years. He carries it, holds it in."

Likely as a result, Adam also struggles with several health issues, including anxiety disorders. Adam today no longer has any illusions that his father or mother, who has been out of the picture for years, will be there for him.

When asked what the worst thing was about living with his grandmother, he at first could think of nothing. Then he says, "I guess for other people—not necessarily for me—it might be dealing with the fact that their parents aren't there." But "it doesn't bother me," he adds.

Later, Betty would say about that conversation, "Tonight, sitting here doing this discussion, he said the one thing that I didn't think I'd hear. He said, 'Well, I have a mother and father, you know, but you're [his grandmother] always there. At least it's nice to know there's one person.' So that was very touching, really was."

Recently, Adam has also told a few friends that Betty is his grandmother: "That was a big step for him."

Adam and his peers who are cynical of their parents don't long for or want a friendlike relationship with them. Instead, they prefer to keep their parents at arm's length. As Adam said, "My parents were horrible, so why care if they're not here?"

When Betty asks whether he has anything positive to say about them at all, he answers with a small ironic smile: "Do you?"

While focusing on their parents' mistakes and faults, these youths also often discuss, like Adam, how grateful they are for the opportunity to live with their grandparents. As Melanie, a thirteen-year-old, put it: "I actually have transportation. Somebody that can come to my games on time and . . . one roof for more than a month." Jordan, a fifteen-year-old being raised by his great-grandmother Susanna, says warmly to his great-grandmother, "Without you, only God knows where I would be, and I'm just thanking you for that." Indeed, the title of this book comes from Sarah, age seventeen, telling her grandmother, "I can trust you way better than [my parents] because you've always been there for me."

For these youths, a clear-eyed assessment of their parents' behaviors makes them appreciate the ways in which their grandparents have been there for them. As Jenna says of her grandmother, "I don't even call my mother 'Mommy.' *She's* my mother [pointing to her grandmother] because she's been there for me my whole life. Everything's good, better than if I lived with my mother."

These youths who had very cynical views of their parents, writing them off, also had the highest-quality relationships with their grandparents. In Adam's case, he has come to the clear realization that he cannot rely on his parents. Having written them off, he is able to turn entirely to his grandmother Betty for stability and warmth.

"I don't really know about the best thing," Adam says of life with his grandmother, "but maybe it's just having somebody there for me."

LONGING

In contrast, still other youths long for their parents. These youths retain a hope that they will not only go back to live with their parents someday but be able to have a "normal" life in which their parents provide stability and love. James, age fourteen, is one of those teens.

It was the third time that James's parents had called the state troopers to intervene with James, and everyone was at rope's end. James was the first child of Maria and Chris. James had been born prematurely and had several medical issues, and his mother "didn't know what to do," his paternal grandmother, Elaine, says. His emotional and behavioral problems had escalated over the years, until the day one summer afternoon when the state troopers were once again called.

They arrived to find a neighbor pinning James, age ten, to the ground to control him and his parents hysterical. This time, they threatened to put James "in a facility" and his mother in jail. "And so I looked at her [his mom], and she looked at me, and she said, 'I think it's time you take James,'" says Elaine.

At his grandmother's house, James calmed down for a period, but soon his problems would come roaring back, indicating the depth of what he had been through before coming to Elaine's home.

"I had books thrown at me, chairs," Elaine remembers. "I broke the blood vessels in my arms, but through it all, he always cried and said, 'Nana, I didn't want to hurt you; I was so angry; I was so angry; I've been so hurt. I don't think I'll ever forgive Mommy and Daddy.' He says, 'Nana, have you ever been hit so hard that you can't sit down?' I said, 'No.' He says, 'I have.'"

With better medication and therapy, James would eventually begin to calm down and his outbursts subside. Each week, he looked forward to his father's visit, when the two of them would go out to eat or to the movies. But those visits would eventually fade.

His parents had separated, and his father, Chris, now had a new family of stepchildren. With the new family, the weekly visits trickled to nothing. Eventually, his father stopped coming. James was crushed.

Chris and his new girlfriend live in the same development as James's mother and her children, James's other siblings. When James stays at his mother's home, which he does occasionally, he rides his bike by the mobile home where his dad lives with his new family. According to Elaine, James's father would tell him, "You don't belong here, you belong with Mommy."

"His dad has been a big disappointment to him right now," Elaine says.

His grandmother finds James, now fourteen, watching television frequently these days, to get a glimpse what a "normal" family is like: "He says, 'Boy, Nana, I wish I was in a family like that.' . . . Yeah, he longs for family. I just know that he's watching, [and] he longs for the family unit."

Such longing was evident in his last visit to his mother. When he was about to leave, he turned to her and hugged her for a long time and began to cry.

"I'm glad to see that he's able to shed tears," his grandmother says.

In contrast to youths like Adam, those who long for their parents have not written off their parents' ability to fulfill the parental role. Additionally, unlike youths such as Lila, whose mother is part of her life and has a clearly defined role, those who long for their parents have not settled on an alternative, friendlike role that their parents could play in their lives. This ongoing, yet unfulfilled, desire to have their parents truly be their parents can lead to intense feelings of longing.

ANGRY

Sometimes teenagers' complex feelings toward absent parents emerge as anger. These outbursts are directed toward the person closest at hand—the grandparent. As Ashley describes her behavior when she first came to live with her grandparents, "It was like a tornado. It was bad. I fought with you. I bit you. I was definitely really scared because I didn't really realize I'd actually lost my father, and I wasn't realizing that my mother didn't really care."

April is going through something similar, but she takes her anger out by rebelling. April, now thirteen, came to live with her grandmother Mona when she was three and her sister was just turning six. April's mother, Karen, was unable to care for the children, and the situation was turning dire. "She was just sleeping on the couch all day," Mona says of Karen, "and the kids were doing whatever they wanted to do." The five-year-old "was actually cooking breakfast for April, trying to take care of her," Mona says.

Mona stepped in to take the children, but Karen was not happy about it. "The mother was fighting with me, and to this day, she tells them that I took them from her," says Mona.

Things were going fairly well until the girls hit their preteen years and began to rebel. Karen, says Mona, "was always interfering then." Mona and April fought about spending and curfews and other restrictions—and still do. April loves to shop and buys only the best, but she spends too much in Mona's eyes, and they are constantly at war about it. Mona says, "Her mom was selling drugs so, sure, she's naming all these brand-name stuff because Mom used to buy her all this stuff, you know, and I told her I can't do it."

Eventually, Mona resorted to showing the girls the court papers that outlined the abuse and neglect they had gone through. April remembered the neglect, Mona says, but she didn't want to acknowledge her mom's version of the story.

"She was very upset and, you know, ran off up to her room crying and everything, and I went up there and said, 'You know something, you needed to see those papers,' because she didn't want to believe anything because naturally they want to believe their mom. It's hard," says Mona.

Currently, Karen is incarcerated for drug-related crimes. April wants to visit her mother in jail "so she can yell at her," Mona says. "But I don't think it's a place for children," so she has not taken her to visit.

April's mother's calls to April have dwindled, and April doesn't understand how her mom can be so distant. Mona recalls, "I says, 'Your mom had you, that's your mom, you'll always love your mom, but she doesn't know how to be a mom.'"

"The hardest thing," says April, "is, like, really thinking about why your parents couldn't be there. And, like, dealing with all that. And it's, like, a lot of stress once you really think about it."

April may have turned away from her mother, but "her dad she was very close to." Unfortunately, says Mona, "he's same thing. He hasn't seen her in a year."

He, too, is incarcerated and gives the girls "no acknowledgment at all," Mona says. After eleven years, he recently sent April a letter—filled with pictures of his new family.

"She was very upset about that, you know, and I told her [to] write a letter back, tell him how you feel. She hides a lot of stuff, which is why she has this difficulty of letting go [of] a lot of things," says Mona.

As shown in chapter 1, a key reason that youths come to live with their grandparents is because their parents voluntarily gave them up. In our analysis, we found that those whose parents gave them up voluntarily were most likely to express feelings of anger toward their nonresident parents. During the teenage years, increasing awareness and feelings of rejection that result from such a situation leads to outbursts of anger. This may be compounded by the fact that often children's nonresident parents, like April's father, have moved on to other partners and to have other children whom they are raising. For example, 80 percent of children in this sample had siblings living outside of their household. As children in grandfamilies get older, it becomes harder to swallow the bitter pill of seeing their parents build a new life with new children, while at the same time, they remain with their grandparents.

Spillover into the Grandparent–Grandchild Relationship

A key concept of family research is that the actions of one family member can reverberate throughout the family to affect others.[3] In the case of grandfamilies, the relationships that youths have with their absent parents can spill over to influence their relationships with the grandparents who are raising them. Looking through the data I gathered from grandfamilies in New York, I found that the quality of the relationship we observed between the grandparent and grandchild, which was assessed based on watching the video interactions, varied depending on the type of relationship the teenager had with the absent parent.

For example, as illustrated at the start of this chapter, Lila and Patty have what they describe as a good relationship with Lila's mother, Nina. They are all clear that while Lila's mother plays an important role in their lives, Patty is the caregiver, while Lila turns to Nina for what is described as a friendlike relationship. Lila, Nina, and Patty get together often and get along well, with each seemingly comfortable in their respective roles. This, in turn, allows Lila and Patty to have clarity about—and strengthen—their relationship. This can be seen in the loving and glowing way that they look at each other and talk about each other during our interview, with Patty telling Lila "you're my rose" and Lila saying with a laugh and a smile that "I do love you guys. . . . It's pretty awesome living with you."

Those who had ambivalent feelings toward their parents, for example, tended to have a lower-quality relationship with his or her grandparent, as well as a higher level of anger. As described earlier, Mona and her fourteen-year-old granddaughter, April, have been having very difficult conversations about April's parents and the reasons April came to live with Mona. These difficulties also seem to play out in a very difficult relationship between April and Mona themselves. For example, April and Mona were unable to find enough to talk about to fill the twenty-minute videotaped segment of the interview. They frequently called us in to cut their discussion segments short, saying they ran out of things to say to each other. When they did speak, there was a great deal of tension and a lack of ability to see each other's side. When April discussed the fact that she would like her curfew to be increased, Mona immediately states, "I need to know where you are at all times, and I need for you to be home at the time I tell you to be home," with April responding "You're a stalker," "You're a mean person," and, speaking to the camera, saying "She owns me" and half-jokingly saying that she is going to call the cops on Mona.

Lindsey, whose story opened the book, and her great-grandmother, Lucille, also had been going through a rough spell in their relationship. Lindsey was chafing at Lucille's restrictions, and Lucille was bewildered at times about teen life today, worried that Lindsey was falling into the wrong crowd and staying out too late.

Lindsey had been in Lucille's care since age three. Her mother, Angie, was sixteen when she had Lindsey and not ready to be a mother, according to Lucille. Angie would leave

Lindsey at Lucille's house and disappear for a few days. The baby was often sick or showed other signs of neglect.

So Lucille stepped in: "I said, OK, give me custody of her for until you get yourself together." Lindsey agreed and Lucille gained temporary custody. "And thirteen years later, I still have her," she says. "She didn't come back for her." Later on, with hindsight, Angie would admit to Lucille that she just hadn't been ready: "She said, 'I didn't want to raise Lindsey doing the things that I was doing, so that's why I left her with you.'"

Angie continued to visit because "I didn't want to keep her from her," says Lucille. Lucille was attuned to Lindsey's longing for her own mother, because Lucille herself was raised by grandparents: "My mom just gave me up when I was little for no reason. So I put myself in her position, you know. I wanted my mom, and I know the feeling, so that's why I couldn't adopt her. I think that would have been one of the worst mistakes I could have made because I feel like children should be with their parents."

As Lindsey hit her teen years, she wanted to spend more time with her mother, who lives nearby. Yet Lindsey has not skirted the confusion and conflicted feelings of being "given up" like that. And those feelings have led to struggles.

"She can strike out at you, and I realize that," Lucille says of Lindsey. "I think with her it's because she wants to be with her mom. It's not so much she's striking out at me. She's angry at me because she feels like I took her from her mom, and I understand that."

Lindsey later would tell Lucille during an interview, "It's always going to be inside of me. You know, I thank God for you guys trying to help us and—but our state of mind is still going to be always 'This isn't my mom.' Reality. Face it."

That reality, Lindsey admits, is difficult: "I remember when I was younger, I used to call you my parent. And then when I got older, I'm thinking 'This is not my mom.' You know? If you sit down and think about it, it's so upsetting."

Now that she is older, she questions what role Lucille plays in her life, which not only leads her to reflect more deeply on the limited role her mother is able to play in her life but also hinders the relationship she has with Lucille. As a result of this ambivalence, Lindsey sometimes feels as though she doesn't really have to listen to Lucille, since she is not her "real" parent.

Slowly, though, they are coming to some resolution, and Lucille is working to listen more and dictate less.

"At first it was hard to deal with, but right now we have a relationship," says Lucille. But, she says, children being raised by their grandparents all struggle at some point: "I can understand what they going through. It's not that because they bad kids; it's just because they miss their parents. And if their parents realized this now, if they know what these children were going through, they would straighten up."

The questioning and pain that such ambivalence creates suggests that a clearly defined relationship with the absent parent, even if it is a somewhat negative one, may be adaptive for teenagers in grandfamilies, while those who feel simultaneously drawn toward and pulled from their parents may experience a lack of role clarity, with repercussions for the youths' well-being as well as the relationships with the grandparents.

Perhaps for this reason, many grandparents go out of their way to engage in strategies designed to "bond" their grandchildren with the absent parents. This, however, can often be an uphill battle.

Edie is trying to encourage her granddaughter, Brittany, age fourteen, to at least write to her mother or answer her repeated phone calls.

"I really don't want to," Brittany says, eyes downcast. "My birthday's coming up. Maybe she'll actually call me. But I doubt it."

"Why not answer?" Her grandmother nudges.

"I don't want to talk to her," Brittany responds.

"Just let her say, 'Happy birthday,' to you, Brittany," her grandmother replies.

"That's what I have voice mail for," retorts Brittany.

"That's not nice," says Edie.

"She already knows that I don't want to talk to her," Brittany says. "It's pretty obvious, isn't it? She knows I was angry with her."

"But why do you hold a grudge? That's no good. Life is too short, baby. You've got to forgive and forget," Edie suggests.

"I don't like her," Brittany snaps.

Despite such resistance, grandparents persist in bringing the family together. As one grandmother describes her efforts: "She [her granddaughter] wasn't talking to her mother, and the mother wasn't talking. But I bond them back. It took twice, but I did it. I bonded them together."

In contrast, it was extremely rare for us to observe instances in which the grandparent attempted to negatively influence the teenager's relationship with the absent parent or drive a wedge between the two. A large research literature on the well-being of children with divorced parents illustrates how children can suffer if their parents bad-mouth each other. This research highlights the importance of parents, despite living apart, working together in the best interest of the child.[4] Given this evidence, the fact that grandparents appear to go above and beyond to keep channels of communication open between their grandchildren and their absent parents is reassuring and highlights a key strength of such families. At the same time, the involvement of nonresident parents in children's lives can cause difficulties, including sadness for the children, as well as challenges for the grandparent–grandchild relationship. As such, a grandfamily faces a difficult balancing act in determining whether and how to incorporate the absent parent into their family life.

Conclusion

As this chapter shows, despite not living in the household, parents can and do play key roles in the lives of grandfamilies. Youths in grandfamilies often live near their parents and remain in contact with them, even if that contact is sporadic. Additionally, the choices parents made and their behaviors reverberate in ways that influence grandparents, parents, and grandchildren alike. When parents voluntarily give up their children, yet live nearby and have even gone on to have other children, this can cause great strain in parent–child relationships, raising obvious questions in the minds of the teenaged grandchildren as to why they are not living with their parents when their other siblings are. Additionally, parental substance abuse, which often goes along with erratic and violent behavior, makes it very challenging to develop healthy parent–child relationships. On the other hand, in some cases—such as Estelle's family—parents, grandparents, and children work hard to overcome past hurts and build healthy relationships with each other, with each family member having clarity about the roles they play in each other's lives.

Youths' feelings about their absent parents span a wide range of sentiments, including friendly, cynical, angry, and ambivalent. These strong emotions often spill over to influence the grandparent–grandchild relationship. In our interviews with grandparents and grandchildren, we saw very high levels of warmth and expressions of love; these were most likely to be found among grandparents and grandchildren who had come to some clarity about the roles that the absent parents play in their lives. In many cases, that clarity meant a clear, if harsh, recognition of the limited roles the parents could play in their lives. For other grandfamilies, our interviews were characterized by strain, lack of communication, and, sometimes, anger. This was most likely to occur in families that were still struggling with the questions of how and why their living situations came to be and what roles the absent parents can and should play in their lives.

Therefore, one can think about the parent–grandparent–grandchild dynamic as an interconnected circle, in which each one influences the other. Oftentimes parental involvement in family life can make the grandparent's role more challenging, as seen when parents defy grandparental rules or when the anger youths feel toward their parents is targeted toward the grandparents. Other times, however, the difficulties youths experience with their parents cause them to appreciate their grandparents even more. Despite these challenges, grandparents often go out of their way to keep the parents involved in their lives, understanding that, no matter how important a role they play in their grandchildren's lives, nothing can take the part of a parent.

5

Policies and Programs to Address Grandfamilies' Needs

As indicated in the previous chapters, grandfamilies face a variety of needs specific to their unique living arrangement. This chapter describes these needs, as well as policies and programs designed to address them. In doing so, I highlight some existing policies and programs that meet grandfamilies' needs, as well as identify areas where greater supports are needed.

Many of the programs and policies targeting grand-families vary depending on the legal relationship between the grandparent and grandchild.[1] Therefore, I first review the different types of legal relationships those in grandfamilies can experience.

Legal Landscape

The legal landscape for grandfamilies evolves over time and also varies across states. My discussion here focuses on the legal landscape as of the writing of this book (2017) and in the state of New York, based on information provided by New York's Office of Children and Family Services.

INFORMAL ARRANGEMENTS

In an informal arrangement, a grandchild comes to live with a grandparent with no court order in place and without the involvement of a social service agency. Such families are often not involved with any caseworkers or social service agency and, because they are outside of the purview of any kind of social service system, are often not easily followed or identified. Because of this, data on the frequency of informal grandfamily arrangements are scarce. According to a 2002 report from the Urban Institute,[2] however, the vast majority of U.S. grandfamilies live in informal arrangements. In such arrangements, the grandparent does not have legal custody of the grandchild; custody remains with the biological parents, who retain all rights related to the child unless they give the grandparent authority to make certain decisions (such as those that are education or health related). Grandfamilies in informal arrangements are entitled to receive what are called "child-only" cash welfare payments under the Temporary Assistance for Needy Families (TANF) program. Through the child-only program, cash assistance is provided to nonparental caregivers regardless of caregiver income or resources. Grandfamilies living in informal arrangements are also entitled to Medicaid, if income and other eligibility requirements are met.

DIRECT PLACEMENT CUSTODY

In direct placement custody, the Department of Social Services is involved in removing the child from the parental home and turns to grandparents for placement of the child. Such arrangements are seen as temporary, with the Department of Social Services making regular visits to monitor the living situation and with permanency hearings occurring regularly until the child either returns to the parental home or moves into a more permanent arrangement with the grandparent or elsewhere. During this temporary period, the grandparent is given temporary authority to make decisions for the child, and the child is eligible to receive child-only TANF and Medicaid (the latter if income eligible).

LEGAL CUSTODY OR GUARDIANSHIP

With legal custody or guardianship, the grandparent takes a more active role in seeking custody of the child. The grandparent files a petition in family court and, if approved, receives legal authority to care for the child, including making educational, health, and other decisions. If the child's parents turn over custody, then the grandparent does not need to return to court again; however, parents can force a return to court if they change their minds. If the parents do not agree to turn over custody, the grandparent will need to convince the court that extraordinary circumstances exist that warrant the grandparent being granted custody. When a grandparent has legal custody or guardianship, the birth parents retain some rights and are able to request visitation or a return of custody via the family court system. This can lead to repeated court visits, as described in some of the previous chapters. Like the other arrangements, grandfamilies with legal custody or guardianship are eligible to receive TANF and Medicaid (the latter if income eligible).

KINSHIP FOSTER CARE

A child enters into kinship foster care when the Department of Social Services has found evidence of abuse or neglect in the parental home; the child is removed from the parental home with full custody given to social services, and the grandparent comes forth as someone who is willing to serve as a foster parent. As with all types of foster care, this arrangement is seen as temporary, with the ultimate goal being that the child will either return to the parental home or else be adopted. During the time that a child is in foster care, the Department of Social Services retains custody of the child and is involved in making major decisions about the child. Grandparents who wish to be foster parents must be approved by the state as foster parents and meet the requirements for foster parents, including passing a home study and evaluation that examines criteria such as safety, health, character, and ability to provide care. Grandparents (and other relatives) who are foster parents receive monthly cash payments based on the child's age and needs, which are higher than the child-only TANF benefits. Kinship foster families, like all foster families, also receive extra funding for clothing, transportation, and other costs associated with raising children. Such families also receive additional services designed to support youths' transitions out of foster care and into independence, special counseling or other needs, and other services designed to meet the family's needs. Finally, children in foster care are automatically eligible for Medicaid and do not have to meet Medicaid income requirements.

KINGAP

As these descriptions indicate, kinship foster families receive much more extensive social service supports than other types of grandfamily arrangements, including greater cash assistance and access to a wide range of services targeted to the family's unique needs. However, kinship foster care is seen as a temporary living arrangement, with the child eventually either moving back in with the parent or being adopted, by the grandparent or someone else, with complete termination of parental rights. For many grandparents raising grandchildren, neither of those options is ideal: moving back to the parental home is not viable, yet grandparents are hesitant to undertake the process of adopting their grandchildren, as that entails cutting parental ties in a permanent way. Because of this, many grandfamilies are stuck in less generous and more ambiguous legal situations.

To address this conundrum, the KinGAP program was created as part of the Fostering Connections to Success and Increasing Adoptions Act of 2008.[3] The goal of this act was to provide support for relative caregivers, but it also had broader goals, including improving the well-being of children in foster care, increasing incentives for adoption, and providing support for tribal foster care and adoption services.[4] Individual states can decide whether they want to implement KinGAP, with New York being one of those deciding to do so. KinGAP programs are more permanent than foster care but less legally and emotionally burdensome than adoption. Under KinGAP a child can be permanently placed with a relative (such as a grandparent) who has been that child's foster parent for at least six months, when both adoption and the possibility of the child returning to the parental home have been ruled out. With KinGAP, parental rights do not need to be terminated, meaning that the legal process to enter into such an arrangement is much shorter and less complicated, and also meaning that relationships with parents can be continued in some form, if desired. KinGAP families receive the same level of financial support as do those in foster care, including respite care, possible educational funds for children, eligibility for Medicaid, and support for legal assistance. KinGAP applies to situations in which the child has been removed from the home due to abuse or neglect, the grandparent is approved to serve as a foster parent, and both returning home and adoption are not viable options. It provides a middle ground between adoption and the more ambiguous legal situation that many grandparents find themselves in.

In very rare situations, grandparents adopt the grandchildren they are raising, thereby taking on the role of parent in every legal sense. This occurs when parental rights have been surrendered or terminated and when grandparents meet all relevant state requirements of adoptive parents. Such grandparents are not eligible for any financial or other support from the state.

For some grandparents, adoption is not an option, as it involves completely terminating all rights and responsibilities of the parents. For some this involves a severing of ties that would do more harm than good and represents a point of no return in the relationships among the grandparent, grandchild, and parent. As described previously, Lindsey's great-grandmother, Lucille, was adamant about not adopting Lindsey, drawing on her experience as someone who was raised by her grandmother to emphasize that she feels that children should be with their parents.

Needs of Grandfamilies

Those living in grandfamilies have unique needs, including health issues (their own and their grandchildren's), financial struggles, parenting challenges (discipline, rules and expectations, and the like), and legal issues. This chapter shows how these and other issues play out in families and the policies and programs that can help.

HEALTH

One of the top issues grandfamilies face is a striking level of health problems among both grandparents and grandchildren. One-third of the grandparents in this study reported having a disability, defined in my analysis as instances in which the grandparents reported that they were not able to work due to a disability. This is similar to estimates of the United States as a whole, which show that one-third of adults age sixty-five or older have some kind of disability (although not necessarily limiting employment).[5] In contrast, in the United States as a whole, only 6 percent of parents report having a disability. Thus children in grandfamilies are much more likely to be cared for by an adult with a disability than are children living with their parents. In addition, more than one-half of the grandchildren I interviewed were reported to have a health condition limiting their participation in school or other activities or requiring a doctor, medication, or special equipment (see table I.2). This strikingly common pattern of health problems is confirmed in other studies. Using a sample of urban grandfamilies from across the United States gathered in the Fragile Families dataset, Natasha Pilkauskas and I found similarly high levels of health problems among the grandchildren: 25 percent were obese, 20 percent had an attention-deficit disorder, and 10 percent had a physical health limitation.[6]

It is not clear what is behind the high levels of health problems among those in grandfamilies. Due to their age, it is not surprising that grandparents might have more health problems than parents raising children. However, the rates of disability among grandparents in my sample (32 percent) are far higher than those among parents. In addition, some research indicates that even compared with other grandparents, those raising their grandchildren have worse health and higher levels of stress.[7]

It is also not clear why the health of children in grandfamilies is so poor, particularly in regards to issues involving attention-related disorders. It is possible that the trauma that children in grandfamilies have experienced—often at the hands of their parents and typically the reasons they are living with their grandparents—manifest themselves in behavioral issues later in life, as in the case of Jason.

"When I got him, he was so abused that nobody could touch him," says his grandmother Adele. "If you tried to touch him, he'd get sick. It took me two years to get him so he wouldn't throw up for you looking at him."

Jason came to Adele as a baby after child protective services stepped in. Jason's mother was living with a man who, Adele says, was not interested in having a child in the house, especially after Jason's mother became pregnant with twins by him. "And my daughter was going through a lot of emotional trouble at the time," Adele says.

She has tried to seek help for Jason, but his teen years are stirring up new emotions. "I have him in nothing but counseling to get him over this," she says. "It's just, the older he gets, the more he thinks about it."

Trudy and Alicia have a contentious relationship, as Alicia's monosyllabic answers in chapter 3 revealed. Alicia is still angry with her father and her mother, who was judged unfit to care for Alicia and her brother. Alicia's brother is in therapy, and Trudy would like Alicia to begin working with a therapist, but Alicia resists. Lately, as Alicia enters her teen years, her moods are volatile.

"In the last six months," Trudy says of the change, "she's just bitter, and she's mean. I think she really needs to be in therapy, to help her deal with it, to help her express what she's feeling."

Trudy also talks about how her own health problems affect her behaviors, telling her granddaughter, "I know sometimes I don't come off the way I should, but sometimes I'll be not really feeling good, and I get upset. I apologize for that, but my health is not good."

It is also possible that socioeconomic challenges both relate to the complex issues that lead a child to live with a grandparent and negatively influence the health of grandparents and grandchildren alike. Regardless of the cause, what is clear is that grandparents and grandchildren in grandfamilies need resources to support their health.

New York State children in grandfamilies who are eligible based on their income may receive health insurance through Medicaid or via the Child Health Plus subsidized health insurance program. Families with incomes less than 1.6 times the poverty line pay no monthly premiums if they receive Medicaid. Other families do pay premiums based on income and family size.[8] In New York State, any family with household income less than 400 percent of the federal poverty line qualifies for subsidized health insurance. As shown in table I.1, this represents the vast majority of grandfamilies in the United States (89 percent of whom have incomes below that threshold, or $96,000 per year for a family of four). Indeed, more than 70 percent of children in grandfamilies receive public health insurance, suggesting that such programs are doing a good job reaching grandfamilies.[9]

What may be lacking, however, is access to respite care, which could be crucial for those grandparents with health problems who need a break from caregiving to attend to their own health needs. In addition, Medicaid and Child Health Plus may not always provide adequate resources to meet the unique needs of grandchildren in grandfamilies, such as mental health and other behavioral counseling. As described previously, the foster care system (including KinGAP) identifies children with specific health-related needs and provides extra resources for their care. In addition, through the foster care system, grandparents raising grandchildren can receive funds to support respite care, or time away from their grandchildren, as a way to assist their own health and well-being. However, few grandfamilies are eligible for such benefits.

Project Healthy Grandparents, at Georgia State University, represents a promising way of addressing the complex health needs of those living in grandfamilies.[10] This holistic program, focused primarily on lower-income African American grandmothers raising their grandchildren, utilizes a multipronged approach, including monthly home visits over a one-year period by a nurse and a social worker, access to support groups and parenting classes, and referrals for legal services and early intervention programs as needed. Research suggests that this approach leads to improved physical and mental health among grandparents, reduced stress, and increased feelings of social support.[11]

Focusing on the emotional health needs of both grandparents and grandchildren in grandfamilies, another program, the Kinship Care Connection, is a school-based program in which grandparents attend support-group meetings and personalized interventions such as counseling and case management, while elementary-aged grandchildren are provided with mentoring and tutoring weekly or more often, as well as support groups and individual counseling. These services are provided over an eighteen-week period, and results indicate that this approach can lead to increased self-esteem among children and reductions in stress among grandparents.[12]

These two promising programs suggest that interventions to support grandfamilies are most effective when they take a holistic approach that includes physical, emotional, and behavioral health; when they are intense; when they are tailored to the personal needs of both the grandparent and the grandchild; and when they are sustained over time.

FINANCIAL

Another concern, related to access to health care, has to do with families' financial situations. As shown in table I.1, looking across the United States as a whole, the income of grandfamily households is lower than that of other families with children. For example, 35 percent of grandfamilies live below the poverty line (an income of less than $24,000 per year for a family of four), compared to 23 percent of other families with children; similarly, 29 percent of grandfamilies have incomes between 100 and 200 percent of the poverty line, compared to 22 percent of other U.S. families with children.

My study of grandfamilies in New York did not ask about income directly. However, the average household income of the census tract in which the families lived was just under $38,000 per year, or about 1.7 times the federal poverty line. In contrast, the average U.S. household currently earns $53,000 per year, suggesting that the families I interviewed live in much more financially constrained households than the average U.S. family.[13] Additionally, as shown in table I.2, only 24 percent of the grandparents in my sample were employed. This suggests that the vast majority live on a fixed income comprising either disability and/or retirement funds that were likely not intended to support a larger family with children. Indeed, several of the grandparents I interviewed talked about the challenges of raising children, particularly teenagers, on their limited incomes.

Some policies address the financial concerns of grandparents raising grandchildren. Grandparents who are foster parents, or who are part of KinGAP, receive higher monthly cash assistance payments than other grandfamilies. Those who are not part of these programs (the vast majority of grandfamilies both in my study and in the United States as a whole) are eligible for the less generous "child-only" cash welfare payments under the Temporary Assistance for Needy Families program. Such payments occur when children, but not the adults with whom they live, are considered to be eligible for cash welfare assistance. However, very few grandfamilies receive even this assistance. Research on a U.S. sample of grandfamilies shows that only 20 percent of grandfamilies receive TANF child-only benefits, despite the fact that nearly 100 percent should be eligible for such assistance. It is not clear what accounts for such a discrepancy—whether grandparents are not aware of the availability of the TANF benefits, whether they are discouraged from receiving them in some way, or whether they simply choose not to enroll. Even those who do enroll in the child-only TANF grants have minimal contact with other public agencies, beyond receiving their monthly check, meaning that they are not monitored by social service agencies in terms of their needs or well-being.[14] The end result, however, is that grandparents raising grandchildren outside of the foster care or KinGAP systems, which despite recent advances still includes the vast majority of such families, are taking on responsibilities identical to those in the foster care or KinGAP systems but receive much lower levels of financial and other supports for the care they provide. In this way, many grandparent caregivers are part of what could be considered a "second-tier" foster care system. While it is still early for concrete evidence about the effectiveness of the KinGAP program, early evidence shows that the KinGAP program has been effective in providing greater resources and support to grandfamilies who are not part of the foster care system, suggesting that policies such as KinGAP have the potential to reduce such inequalities.[15]

It does appear that, compared to cash assistance, grandfamilies do have greater access to food and nutrition programs. Natasha Pilkauskas and I have found that, in the United States, 42 percent of grandfamilies receive support to buy food through the Supplemental Nutrition Assistance Program (SNAP; formerly food stamps), and 60 percent of grandchildren in grandfamilies take part in the school lunch program.[16] Thus grandfamilies are widely reached through governmental food and nutrition programs. However, given the large financial burdens such families face, more needs to be done to increase access to cash assistance and other programs that can improve families' bottom lines.

COMMUNICATION

With all these complexities in the mix, it is no wonder that grandparents and grandchildren sometimes find it hard to communicate with each other. Such communication is important though. Research shows that open, consistent communication between caregivers and teens can improve family dynamics and reduce risky behaviors among teens.[17] Communication may be especially important in grandfamilies during the teenage years, as it is at this time that youths develop new awarenesses of their unique living situations and new questions about them. This involves thinking through how and why they came to live with their grandparents, why their living situation is different from that of their friends, what role parents play in their lives, and how they talk to themselves and others about their living situation. Fortunately, the very strong, warm bonds between grandparents and grandchildren, illustrated in previous chapters, provide an excellent foundation on which to develop programs designed to improve communication patterns.

Cornell Cooperative Extension of Orange County, New York, has come up with an innovative way to facilitate communication in grandfamilies through the Family Portraits Project.[18] This project involves grandparents and grandchildren in a six- to ten-session series using art, writing, photography, and computer technology to develop a personal family book. This provides youths with a safe, fun, and educational way to explore their family dynamics and history while improving communication with their grandparents.

The series uses the process of storytelling to allow youths to learn more about themselves and communicate that knowledge to their family members and their peers. At each session, teenagers meet together to discuss prompts that suggest pages in the family book, and discussions ensue on topics such as "the day I was born," "something you should know about me," "my family's biggest challenge," or "the family member I am most like." At the same time, grandparents meet separately to discuss similar topics in a support-group setting. Finally, teenagers and their grandparents come together to work on the book itself. Families take photos, gather existing photos, and pull together other documentation that tells their stories.

At the end of the sessions, participants share their books with each other in a "gallery of books." Each personalized book is a way for teenagers to understand and tell their own stories and how they change over time and is shared with others in order for youths to practice telling their stories with pride. Cornell Cooperative Extension of Orange County has found that the Family Portraits Project allows grandfamilies an opportunity to develop critical communication skills while at the same time developing and telling their unique family stories.

Sally and Heather have developed strong communication skills that programs like the Family Portraits Project foster. The two had a productive discussion about dating, which Heather is more than ready to do, though Sally is hesitant. "You're only fourteen," she says.

"But it's time for me to experience!" Heather cries. Then she reassures her grandmother: "I mean, it's not like I'm going to kiss him or anything, like. I'm not ready for that.

Like, seriously. I want to take it slow, like. I'm scared. I mean, I'd hold hands with him and hug him, but kissing, like, that's a big step."

"Well, I'm glad of that," Sally says. "OK, I agree. Maybe I should start letting you go out."

"Thank you," Heather replies.

"But it would be on a Friday night. Not during the week, on school nights," Sally cautions.

"What about parents?" Heather asks. "Do parents have to come with us?"

"Yeah. For the first few times. I agree," Sally decides.

"All right," Heather concedes. "I can live with that."

Through programs like the Family Portraits Project, other grandfamilies can learn how to tackle difficult communication challenges through listening, dialogue, and respect.

PARENTING

Grandparents raising grandchildren also face challenges related to parenting. Effective discipline strategies can be difficult, and grandparents sometimes struggle with how much to monitor their teens, including keeping up with their friends, how they're doing in school, their online activities, and other behaviors. They must adapt their parenting to the times, in some ways forgoing how they parented the first time around, and work to keep warm, open communication going in the rocky adolescent years. Research shows that, on the whole, warm but firm parenting, often called "authoritative" parenting, is associated with positive outcomes for teenagers, providing chances for youths to make some decisions about their lives but do so within a set of limits and guidelines provided by caregivers.[19]

As shown previously, some grandparents feel the need to protect and guide their grandchildren, though the teens often feel that they are being overprotective. Others crack down on their grandchildren with strict rules in a desire to keep their grandchildren from making the bad choices that their parents made. Still others feel badly about the difficult experiences their grandchildren have had and spoil them instead.

Cornell Cooperative Extension has developed an award-winning curriculum, called Parenting a Second Time Around (PASTA), that addresses many of these concerns.[20] This eight-session program includes information about child development, discipline, how grandparents can care for themselves, living with teens, and how to best connect with parents and other family members.

My colleagues and I have evaluated the PASTA curriculum, finding evidence that those who take part in the program report reduced stress, increased ability to meet their grandchildren's needs and address their behavior, increased communication with and about their grandchildren's parents, and increased knowledge of their legal options.[21] Grandparents taking part in the program report positive outcomes, saying that "I found out I am not alone with what is going on in my family life" and "it helped me be more understanding with my grandchildren."

Programs like PASTA not only offer grandparents raising their grandchildren with an opportunity to come together with others in a similar situation but also provide them with a chance to "brush-up" their knowledge of modern parenting practices.

LEGAL

Not surprisingly, given the complicated and numerous legal arrangements facing grandfamilies, legal issues are a key challenge. As the description of the legal landscape previously indicates, grandfamilies reside in a wide range of legal arrangements, many of which are not permanent and may involve repeated negotiations with parents regarding who has various rights. They may also involve repeated visits to court, which are costly in both time and money.

Recent years have seen improvements in this area, and New York has been a leader in developing innovative policies for grandfamilies. The KinGAP program, described earlier, gives grandparents an option that has the financial benefits of foster care but is more permanent, without needing to go through the legal and emotional hurdles of undertaking adoption. The same law that created the KinGAP program, the Fostering Connections to Success and Increasing Adoptions Act of 2008, also established funds to assist states in creating Kinship Navigator Programs, which help grandparents and other caregivers access resources, including information about legal options and rights.

Despite these advances, grandparents still must be extremely proactive when advocating for themselves and their grandchildren within the legal system, something that requires a great deal of time and resources, both financial and emotional. Paula describes the great lengths she went to ensure that her granddaughter Erin's biological father would not have any legal rights regarding her, gathering detailed information to bring to court hearings.

"I went to everywhere that he had been arrested," she says, "and every jurisdiction that he had been arrested and every crime that he had committed because if this man is recognized as a biological father, he would have rights. For me to bring these kids to see him in some prison somewhere, that was the last thing I wanted to do."

The repeated visits to court and added scrutiny cause some grandparents to walk on eggshells. Estelle describes how she makes an effort to keep her grandson Michael's mother involved in some of the decisions she makes about him and his sisters, so it won't come back to haunt her: "I like to make the decision together with her, because one time when I had to go to court for the girls, I got accused of a lot of stuff that weren't true."

Nora, Matthew's grandmother, describes the emotional and financial drain that comes from repeated visits to court with her son, who repeatedly seeks custody of Matthew. She says of these visits, "It was really, really overwhelming. Every time he got a new girlfriend, every time he got a new wife, we went to court." Financially, too, it nearly broke her.

At the time, she says, like many grandparents, she was unaware of her legal rights, including the right to a court-appointed attorney: "I think that if grandparents actually knew where exactly they stood when applying for a lawyer or talking with a judge, that might be helpful."

Sandra, Laura's grandmother, was also confused about the legal process. "It's strange," she says, "because you don't know in the beginning what you should sign up [for]. You go for legal custodianship, but maybe you should have gone for kinship foster care."

Other grandparents are very prepared and proactive in court and are able to quickly come to a permanent legal status. As described in chapter 2, Tara's grandfather John quickly realized he needed to get custody of Tara: "And we were very fortunate that we had some good and understanding people there [legally], and we've had permanent custody ever since."

Similarly, Lisa "immediately went into action" when she heard that her grandson Patrick's other grandmother was physically abusive toward Patrick and his sister. His maternal grandmother had been caring for the two siblings ever since her daughter had left them as infants.

Lisa says, "I got everything from reference letters from my job, my church, affiliations, the whole nine yards, so, when I went down in front of the judge, all of that was intact. It took one month from the time they called me to the day the judge stamped on the papers 'you have full custody.'"

Darla was able to draw on her network of social-worker friends to help when tragedy struck her family. At age twenty-five, Darla's oldest daughter, Tameka, was murdered, leaving behind a daughter, age nine, and son, age four. Darla took custody of the two children, though not without a fight first. The children's estranged father surfaced during Tameka's murder trial to seek custody of his son, Anton, but not his daughter, Danielle.

"So we were not only faced with the murder trial," Darla says, "but I was also faced with a custody battle, given my grandson."

The father sent the police to her house to take the children.

Darla was living in a two-bedroom apartment at the time, and the father claimed that Anton and Darla's daughter were all sleeping in the same bed, inappropriately.

Darla says, "In court he accused me of allowing my seventeen-year-old daughter and my grandson to sleep together, but at that time after losing my daughter, it was like whatever got us to sleep. And at that time in court, I couldn't hold my head up and explain that."

"We didn't even have time to grieve because I was faced with that custody battle. But I knew a lot. I worked at a health center, had a lot of social workers as friends. I wrote up my own petition, took it to court that day, and got my grandson back. A couple of months later, I won sole custody," she says. "I just thought it was so cruel for his father to use that against us. But I proved him wrong. . . . I closed on a home, and I got a home for my grandchildren."

Fighting with their own children for what they feel is in the best interest of their grandchildren is sad and complicated and creates an adversarial relationship between the grandparents and their own children. For some, fights center on money, with grandparents being accused of seeking custody only to get financial support and parents being asked to pay child support.

Karla, Chrystal's grandmother, feels that the legal system gives biological parents too many chances. Her grandchildren's mother had been charged with child endangerment for the second time, and she was tired of the repeated legal battles. "The law's too lenient on the parent. Gives them too many chances," she says. "Parents shouldn't be allowed to continue to harm their children mentally if they don't want to be a part of their children's lives. It shouldn't take fifteen months for the courts to say, 'You're not a parent.' As far as I'm concerned, you have a month. If you can't be involved in your child's life, then you're not a parent."

Other grandparents are disappointed that their children give up their own children so easily. Edie, Brittany's grandmother, reports, "I got custody, and my daughter gave her up just like that. . . . I didn't want it that way, I wanted us both, you know, fifty-fifty." Indeed, some grandparents go out of their way to allow parents *more* legal rights than the court system mandates. Lucille continues to keep ties alive between Lindsey and Lindsey's mother, Angie, even though Lucille is not legally required to do so. "Even though the judge said no visitation rights, I can't completely keep Lindsey away from her mother. I have to let her go see her mom," she says.

Similarly, Molly acknowledges that she is not legally bound to let her daughter see her granddaughter Erica, "but I try to be nice and let her go" visit her mother.

Conclusion

Great strides have been made in giving grandparents greater legal options and in providing innovative programming for grandfamilies focused on issues such as parenting and communication. The grandparents I interviewed were, in many ways, fortunate to live in New York, which has a history of undertaking innovative policy responses to the complicated living situations of grandfamilies, one prominent example being New York's development of the KinGAP program. Cornell Cooperative Extension, too, has been a leader in developing, testing, and providing programming for grandparents raising grandchildren, including the PASTA program, support groups, youth programming, and other resources. These efforts have, for the most part, been led by advocates, legal experts, and community educators with a strong appreciation for, passion for, the unique strengths and needs of grandfamilies.

Despite these advances, many gaps remain in policies and programs targeting grandfamilies' unique situations. A key issue is lack of access to financial support, with large numbers of grandfamilies not accessing the TANF cash assistance for which they are eligible. More research is needed to understand why this is the case, examining whether it comes from lack of knowledge about the program on the part of grandparents, lack of access, or lack of interest in taking part.

Another important challenge results from the health issues faced by grandparents and grandchildren alike. All service providers working with grandfamilies should be aware of the very high level of health concerns and work to address them as much as possible, including providing respite care for grandparents and giving children access to care that addresses their emotional and behavioral needs.

While some areas offer unique curricula such as PASTA or intensive holistic programs such as Project Healthy Grandparents, many grandfamilies live in communities where such offerings do not exist. Greater awareness of such programs, and the development of new curricula and programs, can address the unique challenges grandfamilies face around parenting and communication.

6

Postscript

Where Are They Now?

Ever since interviewing the grandfamilies who generously gave their time to be part of my study, I have spent months and years analyzing the rich data that I gathered and, while doing so, have often wondered how those families were faring. When I conducted my interviews, in the winter and spring of 2009, the average teenager was fifteen years old, right in the middle of adolescence and just starting to think about the future. I wondered what life held for those youths as they entered into early adulthood and how they and their grandparents were handling that transition. In the spring of 2012, I conducted phone interviews with as many of the original fifty-nine families as I could find. Thirty-one families took part in these interviews and gave me a chance to learn about how their lives had changed, or remained the same, since last we spoke. In these phone interviews, I was only able to interview the grandparents. I asked where the grandchild was living and what the grandchild was doing (school or work), whether the grandparent–grandchild relationship had changed in any significant ways, whether the role of the parents in the family's life had changed in any significant ways, about any other family changes, and whether and how the grandparent and grandchild talked and planned about the future. A few of their stories follow.

Three Years Later

Lindsey and Lucille. When we first interviewed Lindsey and Lucille, Lindsey was struggling with the fact that her mother had left her in her grandmother's care. "Face it," she said about Lucille, who had raised her since infancy, "this isn't my mom." She yearned for a picket-fence family— "Mom, Dad, two kids, and a dog." When she hit her teen years, she'd begun to act out, the ambivalence she felt toward her grandmother—"she's not my 'real' parent"—and her own role as a grandchild being raised by a grandparent casting a shadow on their relationship. Lucille struggled to find the right balance between them. She ensured that Lindsey's mother stayed in the picture, despite having no visitation rights, in part because she knew how important it was for Lindsey. Lucille herself had been raised by grandparents and knew what Lindsey was going through. There was hope, Lucille felt, that they could develop a good relationship with time.

However, shortly after our original interview with Lindsey and Lucille, Lindsey left Lucille's home to live with her mother, and at the time of our follow-up interview, Lucille reported that she had been there ever since. Lindsey is now nineteen years old and, while she did not graduate from high school, Lucille reported that she is training to be a nurse. Lucille was happy for Lindsey to have the chance to get to know and live with her mom and remains in close touch with her—they talk on the phone and get together at least once a week. Lucille reported that she and Lindsey were getting along better now that Lindsey was out of the house. Lucille, at age seventy-seven, also appreciated the fact that she was now living alone for the first time in her life. In this way, Lindsay, Lucille, and Angie came to an arrangement that was working well for all of them.

Andrea and Monica. This pair also opened this book, but unfortunately, they did not respond to our follow-up survey.

Adam and Betty. When we first met Adam, he was fifteen and very cynical about his parents. Adam's father had never wanted a child, going so far as to push his wife, eight months pregnant with Adam, down the stairs. Later he would choke Adam in a fit of rage after stabbing his own brother. Adam's mother had by then faded from his life. As he said of them, "My parents were horrible, so why care if they're not here?" But he did care, and as his teen years took hold, he lost a spark, Betty said: "When he was little, you'd see him smile more in pictures. You never see him smile now." They began to fight more often, frequently over his time spent online, though behind the fighting was a deep and genuine love.

Adam was eighteen and about to graduate from high school when we followed up with Betty, and he was considering attending community college with a focus on something related to the study of animals. As Betty pointed out, this really played to his strengths, as he often preferred the company of animals to people. Overall, Betty said that Adam was worried about the transition to college, but she was proud that he had identified a field in which he could excel.

Adam and Betty, too, had undergone some challenges since our last interview. Betty lost her job and spent six months without work, but she recently had found a new job. That, combined with concerns that she would no longer receive financial support from the state once Adam graduated, left her worried about their finances. Adam took several medications for health issues, including Asperger's, anxiety, and gastrointestinal issues, but Betty reported he was doing a better job taking his medicine than previously. Betty herself had experienced some health problems lately, which reminds Adam that she won't be here forever.

Since the violent incident with his father, Adam has not seen him, though Betty feels that he could benefit from a male role model. He had had sporadic contact with his mother, but they simply didn't have much to say to each other. Betty reported that she and Adam got along very well, as always, and that she appreciated his unique personality. Altogether, she was guardedly optimistic about their future.

Ashley and Nancy. When we first interviewed Ashley, she was fifteen and had been living with her grandparents, Nancy and Frank, for about eight years. Ashley's parents had struggled with drugs, and her father had died as a result of his substance abuse. Ashley had bounced through several foster homes prior to coming to live with Nancy and Frank and always worried that she would be "kicked back out" and return to foster care. When she first arrived at her grandparents, "it was like a tornado," she remembered. "I wasn't realizing that my mother didn't really care," she said. Despite tensions, especially between Ashley and Nancy, Ashley and her grandparents traveled widely, which was one of Ashley's favorite things about living with them. She also felt that by staying with her grandparents, she remained connected to her father as well. "I still have pieces of my father with me," she said. Perhaps because of her early trauma, Ashley's teen years were "defiant," her grandmother reported, and Nancy struggled to find a nice balance with Ashley.

At the time of the follow-up interview, Ashley was eighteen. While Ashley was still officially living at home, she and Nancy had undergone some major changes. Nancy's husband, Frank, had passed away, leaving Nancy and Ashley alone in the house. In addition, Ashley's worry that she would return to foster care had come true. She had spent a year in foster care and had only moved back into Nancy's house eight months prior to our follow-up interview. According to Nancy, this came about because Ashley had become uncontrollable, and she felt she had no choice but to relinquish her parental rights and send her to foster care under state supervision. A variety of social service agencies were involved in this move, and prior to Ashley's return, she and Nancy agreed on a set of rules to follow. At the time of our interview, Ashley and Nancy had fought because Ashley violated a rule about having her boyfriend over, and as a result, Ashley had been staying with a friend for about three days. Overall, Nancy expressed significant concerns about Ashley, reporting that she had missed a lot of school lately and was having a hard time getting out of bed. Ashley was seeing a therapist, but Nancy was concerned that she was depressed. Despite this, Ashley had been doing well in school, and Nancy envisioned her attending community college. Unlike most other families interviewed, Nancy had significant money saved for college and was not concerned about paying for it. Rather than financial issues, Nancy's concerns revolved around Ashley's emotional well-being and their ability to develop a healthy relationship.

Stephen, Jeanne, and Bob. Like Monica and Andrea, we also have no follow-up information on Stephen and his grandparents Jeanne and Bob, who also opened this book.

Lila and Patty. During our first set of interviews, it was apparent that Lila and her grandmother Patty were very close. Lila said frequently how lucky she felt to have grandparents who loved and cared for her. Lila was a very social girl, always participating in after-school programs, playing sports, riding horses, and surrounding herself with a circle of friends. She was also on good terms with her mother, Nina, and seemed to have resolved the relationship well. Her father, on the other hand, had faded from her life, and she was all right with that as well. She had said during the interview that she would have her grandfather give her away at her wedding.

At the time of the follow-up interview in 2012, Lila was eighteen years old. She was a senior in high school and, having been accepted to five colleges, was deciding where to spend the next several years. Patty was hoping Lila would stay close to home, but Lila was thinking otherwise. Patty reported that Lila hadn't seen or communicated with her father since the last interview but that she continued to see her mother every weekend and that they continue to have a sisterlike relationship. Patty's relationship with Nina had improved recently, and they, too, get together once a week, strengthening what had been a difficult mother–daughter relationship. Patty reported that she and her husband would be paying for Lila's college and were the ones guiding her decision-making on this. Although Lila sometimes talks about her college choice with her mother, her mother is not involved in financing it. Overall, Patty felt that Lila's future was very bright, with the small exception of some health problems that had led Lila to stop doing one thing she really loved: playing sports.

I also gathered information on some of the other families whose stories make up this book.

James and Elaine. James had settled into his grandmother Elaine's life when we first talked with them. His start in life had been rocky, with severe behavior disorders, and his parents frequently called the police to intervene. James's anger would spill over to his grandmother at first, throwing books and chairs at her until she could calm him down. With time, the outbursts waned, and James began to settle into his new home. However, he continued to long for his father, Chris, who had remarried and started a new family, leaving James behind. James couldn't quite let go of his father or his dream of being included in a large family, along with his own siblings, who had stayed with their mother. When we last talked with him, James had the habit of watching television in order to get a glimpse of what a loving family was like. James and his grandmother had a close relationship, she said, and she wasn't sure she was ready for the day when he would leave her. "Yeah," she said, "that's going to be very hard for me. But I mean, that's part of it."

When we caught up with James and Elaine, James was about to turn eighteen, finishing high school, and was in a serious relationship with a girlfriend. In the intervening years, he had been diagnosed with bipolar disorder and was doing fairly well at the moment, after a rocky year before. When he was seventeen, he'd become aggressive and threatened a teacher, which led to his hospitalization for two weeks to get his bipolar disorder under control. It was the worst thing she has ever gone through, Elaine told us, but "we made it through." James is currently in therapy every morning at an adolescent treatment program. He also sees a counselor.

His relationship with his grandmother has only deepened over the years, Elaine says, though her own health has deteriorated, and she is worried about the future. She has had two major surgeries "and almost didn't pull through," which worried James immensely because he does not want to live with his mother. His mother has recently married again, this time to a much younger man, only a few years older than James. James is increasingly estranged from her and his other siblings, and they hadn't seen one another for several months at the time of the follow-up interview. "I think the situation is starting to sink in for James," says Elaine, referring to the fact that he was finally letting go of his dream of building a relationship with his mother and siblings.

James's father, whom he pined for at our earlier interviews, had recently come back into his life. He, too, had married again, and his new wife wanted him to be involved with his children. He has been taking James to the racetrack and is spending more time with him. They also text almost every day, his grandmother reports. The blossoming relationship has been very good for James, Elaine says.

James hopes to get a job in the near future, and his girlfriend is trying to persuade him to become a bus driver, though Elaine thinks that will be impossible with his mental health issues. She doesn't see him moving out any time soon, she says, thinking that he will need more time before he is ready to fully launch into adulthood.

Amanda and Tony. When we first met Amanda and her grandfather Tony she was fifteen. Tony, at age sixty-one, had reluctantly taken her and her brother in because their mother was addicted to drugs and could not care for the children. Tony is gruff but a softie underneath. During their joint interview, he and Amanda had tussled over dating, which Tony was adamantly opposed to. "I know exactly what's going through that guy's head," he'd told her, "whether he says it is or it isn't."

He'd had Amanda and her brother officially for two years when we conducted the interviews, though they had been in and out of his life since they were born. His daughter was in rehab at the time of the interview, and Tony was conflicted. He wanted his daughter to kick her drug habit, but he also realized that meant he would lose Amanda and Riley. "It might be a good feeling, I don't know," he had said. "It sort of changed your whole life, and now if they're not living with me anymore, I got to go adjust back to being a regular person."

In the end, he would never have to face that prospect, as his daughter never kicked her habit. She was still using at the time of the follow-up interview, and unfortunately, so was Amanda. Tony told us that Amanda's drinking had started in high school, and she had been to rehab twice since. Tony isn't sure if she's an alcoholic or if she "just drinks because her friends do." Despite these challenges, Amanda did graduate from high school and has started community college and is considering becoming a drug counselor herself, though as Tony says, she changes her mind frequently. She wants desperately to live independently and recently moved out to give it a try, though, Tony says, "it was too much for her." She moved back in but continues to talk of moving out again.

She and Tony are still close, though he says they are not as close as they once were. "There are lots of things she doesn't tell me, like about the boys she goes out with who aren't too nice," he says. He admits that he will likely never see her as a grown woman because, he says, "[it's] hard to picture her as anything but a little girl." He hopes that she will begin to make more healthy choices to lay the groundwork for her future.

Tara and John. Tara's mother also struggled with drug abuse. Tara was just over two years old when she came to live with John, age sixty-six, and his wife. Their daughter gave them an ultimatum: take Tara or I drop her off at social services. "It was dumped in our lap," he'd said, but "it changed my life completely, in some ways positively."

Tara had not seen her mother but a handful of times since she had moved in with her grandparents. When we had first interviewed them, John was extremely proud of Tara, who was age eleven at the time. She spoke regularly at their church and was an outgoing and personable young woman. For her part, Tara loved her grandfather and realized how lucky she was, saying that her grandparents' maturity was a huge advantage. "Parents in their thirties," she says, "don't know anything because usually they're young and they're not smart."

When we caught up with them again, Tara was sixteen, a freshman in high school and on the honor roll at school. John, who at the original interview had lamented that his health prevented him from doing active things with Tara, had recently had a health scare but was recovering. John was now seventy-one, and he said that Tara recognizes that she must help out more, which she is happy to do.

Her relationship with her grandparents is still strong, though entering the teen years, John realizes, won't be easy. "She is thinking she's a young lady, and you can't argue with a child when they're right," he says. "It keeps me on my toes." But he also says that their relationship has grown as she has gotten older, and they now can communicate in a "more meaningful way," he says. They also both turn to the Bible for guidance when they face challenges, and their church continues to be a strong bond between them. Tara sees her mother sporadically, but "the older she gets, she wants less and less with her mother, because she feels like her mother doesn't treat her right," John says. As for her future plans, Tara has her eyes on a trade school, and John is hoping that there will be some form of financial support because otherwise they will not be able to afford it. "We need our roof to be fixed and other repairs on [our] house," he says. Despite having paid off their mortgage, "we are still not making it month to month. We had some savings but don't have any anymore," John says. He'd also like to take a vacation with Tara, but it is out of the question, he thinks, although he dreams of the possibility that they could take a cruise one day. He remains frustrated about what he feels is a lack of financial support for grandparents.

"Making the decision to take in and raise a grandchild takes a burden off of the government," he says, "but they do not recognize us grandparents. We're not asking for a hand-out, but we need help."

Matthew and Nora. When we first met Matthew and his grandmother Nora, Matthew was sixteen and pushing against the constraints Nora had set. Their video interview ended in a fight over his attitude and his desire to enlist in the military, like his absent father. His father was a veteran who had largely disappeared from Matthew's life, though Matthew held out hope that they would reconnect. He was angry with his dad, but when his dad called, his heart would melt, Nora said. His longing for his father was apparent in his description of what it was like to live with a grandparent. "It's like a banana split without the banana," he said. For her part, Nora was frustrated with Matthew and feeling the burden of caring for a teen. "Well, I don't feel any different than you," she told him. "I feel like it's a never-ending job. And the more that I do, the less you guys appreciate."

When we caught up with them again, Matthew was about to turn twenty, and he and his girlfriend were expecting their first child. Their fights had continued, and Nora, now age sixty-two, had kicked Matthew out because she felt like her only job was to be his maid. Matthew was living with his girlfriend in another city, working at a temporary job. His younger brother, age thirteen, was still living with Nora. Since Matthew has moved out, Nora says, their relationship is better, though she wishes he'd find a more permanent job. It will be hard, she thinks, because he now has a criminal record. Although recognizing he is young, she is excited that he and his girlfriend are expecting a baby. His relationship with his father, however, remains strained. He speaks with his father sporadically, the last time at Christmas when his father visited but then needed money to return home. "There were hard feelings," says Nora. Overall, she feels that there are many unresolved issues when it comes to Matthew's future.

Summary

The stories of these families highlight themes that emerge when looking at the other families with whom we were able to conduct follow-up interviews. Almost all of the grandparents reported that their grandchildren were still living at home. For the most part, this is not surprising, given the young age of the grandchildren, who ranged in age from fifteen to twenty-one at the time of the follow-up interviews. However, there is some evidence that some of the older grandchildren were having a hard time "launching" into independent adult lives. Three grandparents reported that their grandchildren had attempted to move out and go away to college but quickly returned home, oftentimes due to physical or emotional health reasons. Other grandparents of older grandchildren reported that their grandchildren were still home with them, more by default than by choice.

For example, Sherry reported that her granddaughter, Melissa, now age twenty, was living at home and had had a very hard time finding a job. At the time of the follow-up interview, Melissa had just gotten a part-time job, but both she and her grandmother were frustrated that she was still living at home, and this frustration was affecting their relationship. "It is clear," said Sherry, "that she doesn't want to be living here." Holly, who knew her grandparents loved her unconditionally—"Like, you can screw up in the biggest way, and at the end of the day, your grandma will still hug you and say that they love you"—had dropped out of high school and repeatedly fought with her grandparents, who attempted to get her to stay in school or get a job. She eventually left to live with her other grandparents and is neither in school nor working.

Much more common was for grandchildren to be living at home while attending school or college. Several of the older teens had graduated from high school, or gotten GEDs, and were simultaneously working while attending school. For example, Anne, Marsha's granddaughter, was working at a fast-food restaurant while living at home and attending college. In these instances, living at home is not an indication of a "failure to launch" but rather a strategy allowing for grandchildren in families with limited means to pursue their education.

Other grandchildren were at the end of high school and, like Ashley and Adam, were anticipating the next stage in their lives. Sally reported that Heather was doing great in school and considering college options. Sally and Heather had open channels of communication during the teen years, as the conversation about dating in the previous chapter revealed. As noted earlier, Tara is on the honor roll and considering entering a trade program after graduating from high school.

Several grandparents reported that it was easier for them to communicate with their teens at the time of the follow-up interviews, likely due to the increase in maturity among the teens. For some grandchildren, the relationship with the parents was reported to have improved, perhaps because of greater maturity on the part of both the parents and grandchildren. For example, Stacy, who was extremely close to her great-grandmother and knew she could always count on her, saw her mother, LaToya, regularly. LaToya was even paying for part of the costs of college. Similarly, Heather's mother moved in with them, which was going well, Sally reported, for the most part, although they sometimes clashed when the mother wanted to exert parenting authority.

Other grandparents reported that relations with the parents had worsened since the last interview. For example, Mona, who already had a contentious relationship with April's mother, Karen, reported that both of April's parents had lived with them recently. Karen had recently been evicted. The father, who had recently been released from prison after fifteen years and who until then had not acknowledged April except to send her a picture of his other child, needed a place to stay after his release. The living arrangement proved short-lived and difficult. Eventually, Mona had to kick both parents out of her home because they fought constantly and were very unstable.

Almost every grandparent interviewed in the follow-up mentioned increased health problems since the initial interview causing concerns about the future. At the extreme, Paula, Erin's grandmother, reported that she was on oxygen around the clock as her congenital heart failure took its toll. She reported that she did not think she would be alive by the time Erin, aged seventeen, went off to college and that she relied on Erin, still in high school, for the majority of the household duties, including shopping, cooking, and cleaning. Some grandparents reported that their increased health issues made things very difficult for their grandchildren, who face not only the challenges of transitioning to independence but also the potential deaths of the people who have been their caregivers and touchstones for most of their lives. Several grandmothers reported that their husbands had passed away or been very ill, and others mentioned very frank conversations with their grandchildren about what would happen to them if they were to die. Other grandparents mentioned that they were now calling on their grandchildren for care, as their abilities declined (some in wheelchairs or facing other serious medical conditions) and the grandchildren got older.

Some health concerns were related to the grandchildren's physical and mental health. In some cases, a difficult transition to adulthood raised mental health issues. For example, as described previously, Nancy was very concerned about what she perceived as Ashley's severe depression, a symptom of which was her having a hard time getting out of bed. While she was seeing a therapist, Nancy was cautious in her optimism, as several previous attempts at therapy had not, she felt, resolved key issues. In other cases, the high rates of attention-deficit disorders faced by youths in this study made the transition out of the home and to independence difficult. Matthew's grandmother Nora reported that he, at age twenty, had dropped out of college and was in a low-paying part-time job, a dead-end situation that she attributed to his emotional and developmental issues, including post-traumatic stress disorder (PTSD) and attention-deficit disorder. The issue of emotional and mental conditions making it difficult to complete education and get a job was raised by other grandparents as well in the follow-up interviews.

Finally, many grandparents reported concerns about finances. Several mentioned that they were not sure how they would pay for college, with the vast majority indicating that they were not expecting the child's parent to contribute toward college costs. Others mentioned that their eligibility for social service programs changed once their grandchildren started working or turned nineteen, which caused hardship.

Conclusion

I was so grateful for the opportunity to reconnect with many of the families I interviewed in the original study. As with any data-collection project, some families were not able to be interviewed, either because the community agencies with whom we worked to recruit families in the first place had lost contact or because they simply did not want to take part. It is difficult to know if we would have come away with a different picture of the lives of these families had we been able to follow-up interview everyone. It is possible that those whom we did not interview were facing greater challenges than others, and that shades our understanding of how these families fared moving forward, but that would just be a guess.

Looking at the interviews we were able to conduct brings a mixture of happiness and concern. Families such as Lila's, who already had strong relationships, a great deal of warmth, excellent communication, and a clear understanding of each other's family roles, continued to thrive. Others, such as Ashley and Nancy, continued to struggle with the same issues of communication, emotional challenges, and strain that they faced the first time they were interviewed. Some, such as Adam and Betty, face the same challenges as before but continue to do so with a strong undergirding of love and respect, leading to guarded optimism about both of their futures. Some youths entered into a phase of life where big events with long-lasting repercussions can and do occur, such as substance abuse and having children. Many others are embarking on journeys of further education and career exploration.

Taken together, the families I had the privilege of interviewing look like many other U.S. families today—poised on the edge of adulthood, contemplating their futures with a mixture of excitement and uncertainty. What is unique about grandfamilies is that this is done with the added stressors of deteriorating health among many grandparents, very challenging financial constraints in many cases, and continued ambiguity about what role the parents will play as grandchildren enter into young adulthood. At the same time, the love, commitment, and warmth that are endemic to the grandfamilies who shared their stories with me continues. As Sinead, age sixty-eight at our original interview, puts it regarding her grandson: "The older he gets, the better it gets."

Conclusion

I went into this project with the goal of "getting under the roof" of grandfamily households, asking what we know about the complex relationships and circumstances of grandfamilies, how do such families come about and what role do the absent parents play in the lives of children living in grandfamilies, what challenges do grandparents raising their grandchildren face (especially during the teenage years), and what unique strengths and advantages exist in such families. I also wanted to understand which policies and programs might best address these families' unique circumstances and needs. By addressing these questions, I hope to increase our understanding, and appreciation, of the lives of grandfamilies and inform the development of effective policies and programs to address grandfamily needs.

In doing so, I also sought to add to the large body of research on the complexities of modern U.S. family life. While significant progress has been made in illustrating the extent to which family life has evolved beyond the traditional nuclear family over the last several decades, for the most part, this research has not broadened to include children who do not live with their parents at all, particularly those being raised by grandparents.

With these goals in hand, my research team and I undertook a multipronged study of the lives of fifty-nine families in New York State. Weighed down by bags of video equipment, recorders, paper, pens, and laptops, and excited but nervous for what this adventure might bring, we drove across the state, from the most rural corners to the most highly urban areas in our country. A wide range of valuable discoveries emerged from that experience.

On the scholarly side, our careful analysis of the data we collected revealed several important themes relevant to our knowledge of grandfamily life. First, while many factors can lead a child to be raised by his or her grandparent, these families most commonly come about as a result of a voluntary decision on the part of the parent. For many children in grandfamilies, their entrance into a grandfamily occurred as a result of an active choice on the part of their parents, sometimes described as the parents "shoving them by the wayside." At the same time, despite giving up their children, parents play significant roles in the lives of grandfamilies. They often live nearby and remain in contact with their children and the grandparents raising them, even if that contact is sporadic. Some parents choose their romantic partners over their children, oftentimes moving on to have children with those partners, raising obvious questions in the minds of the teenaged grandchildren as to why they are not living with their parents when their other siblings are. Others struggle with mental health and substance abuse problems that result in erratic behavior toward their children. Still others are simply too immature to focus on being a parent.

The behaviors of and choices made on the part of the absent parents have important implications for grandchildren and grandparents alike. Despite oftentimes erratic and difficult behaviors of the parents, many grandparents, grounded in love for their own children, work hard to build bridges with the parents, keeping them involved in the lives of their grand-families and seeking to build healthy relationships among all involved. Thus grandparents often go out of their way to keep the parents involved in their lives, understanding that, no matter how important a role they play in their grandchildren's lives, nothing can take the part of a parent.

Not surprisingly, the feelings that youths express about their absent parents span a wide range of sentiments, including friendlike, cynical, angry, and ambivalent. These strong emotions often find release on the person closest at hand, the grandparent, and can influence the grandparent–grandchild relationship, causing strain. Despite these challenges, many of the interviews we conducted were characterized by very high levels of warmth and expressions of love; these were most likely to be found among grandparents and grand-children who had come to some clarity about the role that the absent parents played in their lives, even if that meant a somewhat harsh recognition of the limited role the parents could play in their lives. For other grandfamilies, we observed strain, lack of communication, and sometimes anger between grandparent and grandchild. This was most likely to occur in families that were still struggling with the questions of how and why their living situations came to be and what role the absent parents can and should play in their lives.

While parental involvement in family life can make the grandparent's role more challenging, as seen when parents defy grandparental rules or when the anger youths feel toward their parents is targeted toward the grandparents, more often the difficulties youths experience with their parents cause them to appreciate their grandparents even more. For some youths, this is as simple as appreciating that they have food to eat and a roof over their heads. For others, this involves a more complex recognition of the ways in which their grandparents had supported them both physically and emotionally.

Teenagers and grandparents in grandfamilies define their roles in relation not only to the absent parents but also to each other. Some grandchildren go out of their way to refer to their grandmothers as "Mom." Others explicitly state the opposite, and the lack of consistency in what name best describes a grandparent in a grandfamily indicates the ways in which such a role can be undefined, potentially causing stress. Regardless, both grandparents and grandchildren express strong feelings of gratitude about the unique roles they are able to play in each other's lives. Indeed, grandchildren in this study went above and beyond to emphasize how much they appreciate the emotional and material support provided to them by their grandparents. Grandparents themselves also appreciate the opportunity to play a special role in their grandchildren's lives and gain a sense of pride and meaning in doing so.

Despite this remarkable grounding in love, warmth, and appreciation, grandfamilies face numerous challenges as well, including ambiguity over who is really the parent, lack of clarity on the legal relationship between the grandparent and the grandchild she is raising, and the difficulties in taking on a parenting role later in the life cycle, or "off time." Overarching all of these is the fact that the role of a grandparent in grandfamily households is often undefined, changing, and surrounded by ambivalent feelings regarding how and why the living situation came to be in the first place.

At the same time, grandparents uniformly feel that the joy and benefits that come from raising their grandchildren outweigh any challenges, however real. These benefits range from the care and companionship that their grandchildren may provide to an increased sense of purpose and engagement in the outside world that they otherwise would not have. Some grandparents find raising their grandchildren an opportunity to redeem themselves from what they see as past mistakes or to simply be the opportunity to raise children again as an older and wiser person with more experience. Others simply appreciate the chance to be a parent again, warts and all. Altogether, grandparents not only gain value from the role they play in caring for their grandchildren but feel that they are making important contributions to society by doing so. Their only complaint is that society often doesn't seem to notice or appreciate their contributions, something this book seeks to address.

Like all teenagers, grandchildren in grandfamilies face the task of creating a coherent narrative of their lives. For these youths, this narrative involves gaining insight as to how and why they came to live with their grandparents and what roles their parents have in their lives. Because of this, issues regarding parents and their roles in the lives of grandfamilies often come to a head during the teenage years. Teenagers living with their grandparents, even those who have been doing so for the vast majority of their lives, may reevaluate their parents' past behavior and current involvement, questioning why they came to live with their grandparents in the first place, what role their parents play in their lives, and how they relate to both their parents and their grandparents. A larger-than-usual generation gap, and anger and confusion about the role of the parent, can make this process even more challenging and can negatively influence the grandparent–grandchild relationship. Grandparents and those who work with them should be prepared to revisit the stories of how and why their families came to be, even if they thought they were resolved. Innovative programs, such as the Family Portraits Project, can help with this process.

Fortunately, teenagers exhibit a remarkable level of warmth, love, and appreciation toward their grandparents, as their grandparents do toward them. This underlying relationship of affection and warmth gives teenagers in grandfamilies an excellent source of strength as they tackle some of the challenges they face.

Some challenges faced by grandfamilies have to do with the lack of financial resources, compounded by the fact that in many families, the grandparents are not working due to either retirement or disability. Another key challenge is the high prevalence of health problems among both grandparents and grandchildren. While it may not be surprising that grandparents' health makes it difficult to keep up with active kids, that doesn't make the issue any easier. What was surprising was the high level of health problems faced by the youths we interviewed, particularly emotional and behavioral issues. This suggests that both grandparents and grandchildren in grandfamilies would benefit from special services designed to identify and treat their unique health needs.

Other issues faced by grandfamilies include the strain of repeated legal battles with the nonresident parents and a larger-than-usual generation gap that causes challenges with parenting strategies. While some promising policies and programs address these challenges, several areas remain ripe for further intervention, including lack of access to financial support and the need for more resources related to parenting and communication in grandfamilies.

This study would not be complete without the opportunity to reconnect with many of the families interviewed in the original study. Like many other U.S. families, these grandfamilies face the excitement and opportunity of young adulthood. Grandfamilies do so under some added challenges, including deteriorating health among many grandparents, financial constraints that limit access to college and other educational opportunities, and continued ambiguity about what role the parents will play as grandchildren enter into young adulthood. While I am not able to follow these families further to see how their lives play out and do not dismiss the difficulties that many of them face or the need for greater supports, I remain optimistic about the ways in which the love, warmth, and appreciation they have for each other paves the way for a healthy future together.

This project also resulted in a great deal of knowledge that was personal, rather than academic. Talking to families who, despite great challenges, clearly and passionately demonstrated their love and support for each other reminded me what it takes and means to be a family. While conducting these interviews meant time away from my own family, I returned from each visit even more grateful than before for my own family bonds. Families come in all shapes and forms, and each one faces challenges, some more than others. I hope that this book leaves others as grateful as I am for the openness and honesty of the New York grandfamilies who opened up their lives to me.

Appendix

Information on Data Coding

Coded Videotaped Data

Three researchers viewed and coded the videotaped data. Tapes were randomly assigned. Each ten-minute video segment was assigned and coded separately. The researchers watched each tape at least two times—once to code for the teen and another to code the grandparent—with the order chosen randomly. Items coded for the grandparent were: anger, communication, depression, dominance, inductive reasoning, listener responsiveness, monitoring, parental influence, validation, and warmth. Items coded for the teen were: anger, communication, defiance, depression, dominance, emotional maturity, listener responsiveness, and warmth. Finally, researchers coded a dyad-based code of overall relationship quality.

The codes were adapted from three sources. First was the Scale of Intergenerational Relationship Quality (SIRQ),[1] which has been used to measure the relationship between teen mothers and their mothers in lower-income, diverse samples. The second source was the Iowa Family Interaction Rating Scales (IFIRS),[2] which were developed to measure the verbal and nonverbal behaviors and communications of individuals and groups of people. All measures were coded on a scale of one to nine (in which 1 = highly uncharacteristic and 9 = highly characteristic). The first two authors double-coded a random set of tapes until consensus was reached (defined as the average discrepancy across five segments being one point or less, representing 80 percent reliability). Once the first two authors reached consensus, the first author became reliable with the third coder. The three researchers then coded the remaining segments. A total of 30 percent of all segments were double-coded, and consensus was reached in instances in which the two coders were greater than one point apart—or when one coder had a one and the other had a two on any scale.

Qualitative Data

The transcribed video and audiotapes were coded to capture the grandparent's and youth's perceptions of the relationship the child has with his or her parent, using Dedoose mixed-method software. In order to determine the concepts for which these transcripts would be coded, the team undertook a detailed process, with a focus on the themes key to this study of relationships in grandfamily households. First, a thorough literature review was used to identify concepts. Next, the first two authors met with a group of community educators who work regularly with grandparent-headed families to further identify concepts of interest to them and the families they serve. A research team of five people then read a random selection of transcripts in order to identify any new concepts and to compare these against those that had already been identified. The team then came up with a preliminary list of concepts and read through two random transcripts to classify overarching categories. The list of concepts was then modified, and a codebook was developed. This codebook was used to code two more randomly chosen transcripts, the team met and came to consensus on coding those transcripts, and the codebook was finalized. Each member of the five-person team coded randomly assigned transcripts and then met with the first author to reach consensus for 20 percent of the transcripts.

The transcribed video- and audiotape transcripts were read and classified into categories representing the *reasons the youth was not living with his or her parent*. Reading through the open-ended questions asked of the grandparent on this topic, we inductively coded several nonmutually exclusive reasons, shown in table 1.1.

The transcribed video- and audiotape transcripts were also analyzed for the following overarching themes and subthemes:

1.0. Grandparent role
    1.1. Grandparent feelings about youth arrival
    1.2. Grandparent view of role
    1.3. Youth view of role
    1.4. Grandparent life changes
    1.5. Grandparent warmth/gratitude
    1.6. Youth warmth/gratitude
    1.7. Youth fear of grandparent death
    1.8. Grandparent on spoiling
    1.9. Youth on spoiling
    1.10. Grandparent thoughts on youth living elsewhere
    1.11. Youth thoughts on living elsewhere
2.0. Parenting
    2.1. Grandparent on discipline/rules/expectations
    2.2. Youth on discipline/rules/expectations
    2.3. Grandparent on technology issues
    2.4. Youth on technology issues
    2.5. Grandparent on generation gap
    2.6. Youth on generation gap

Acknowledgments

First and foremost, I want to thank the families who spent their valuable time educating me about their lives. The trust, honesty, humor, and patience they showed me will forever be appreciated.

This work would not have been possible without generous funding from the William T. Grant Foundation Scholars Program, the purpose of which is to encourage researchers to take a chance on a new research project. I am eternally grateful for the foundation's trust and investment in me. I am also grateful for support and funding from the National Institute of Food and Agriculture Hatch and Smith-Lever funds, Cornell University's Bronfenbrenner Center for Translational Research, Cornell University's Institute for Social Sciences, and an anonymous Cornell University donor. I also greatly appreciate my mentors via the William T. Grant Scholars Program, Lindsay Chase-Lansdale, David Harris, Karl Pillemer, and Laurie Wakschlag, all of whom generously provided their time and extremely helpful insights. I thank Greg Duncan and Sheldon Danziger, whose generous mentorship has been invaluable throughout my career. I also am forever grateful to Alan Mathios, who has shown me how to lead with both strength and kindness.

It took a village to carry out the work presented here, and I am grateful for all who worked with me on this project.

First, special thanks to Kimberly Kopko, who has been with me from the very beginning of this project, drove with me to every corner of New York State, has the words of grandfamilies ringing in her head as well, and remains an excellent collaborator as we continue to understand the lives of these unique families. I also thank my research team, Eliza Cook, Anne Darfler, Maria Korjenevitch, and Emily Sanders, for their excellent and dedicated work.

This project would not have existed if not for the contributions of the Cornell Cooperative Extension parenting educators with whom I have had the privilege of working. These experts in parents and families taught me about the importance of studying grandfamilies, helped me think about the best way to do so, worked with me to collect the data presented here, and have been invaluable in helping me interpret the findings. I would like to thank Denyse Variano, whose patience and expertise are never-ending and have made a huge impact on my life and work. I also thank Linda Coleman, Jackie Davis-Managaulte, Emi DiSciullo, Isabelle Jensen, Diane LaTorrey, and Brenda Reynolds for their dedication to improving the lives of vulnerable families and their excellent collaboration on this project.

Barbara Ray provided essential editorial services, helping the words of the families I interviewed shine through.

Rena Seltzer provided excellent advice and guidance on time management and prioritization, without which this book would not have been completed.

My research on grandparents and the roles they play in children's lives continues in other forms, and I am grateful for my research collaborators, Mariana Amorim, Kelly Musick, Natasha Pilkauskas, Megan Dolbin-MacNab, Chris Near, and Kathleen Ziol-Guest, for our ongoing work together.

Thank you to my generous friends and colleagues, Rob Crosnoe, Amy Howard, Karl Pillemer, Sharon Sassler,

Laura Tach, Maureen Waller, and Chris Wildeman, who gave essential advice about the process of writing a book. I am also very fortunate for the collaborators, mentors, friends, and colleagues who have impacted my research and life in numerous ways: Rosemary Avery, Rich Burkhauser, Marcy Carlson, Kristin Cerione, Ashley Davis, Jean DeMoss, Sandy Dhimitri, Margaret Frey, Christina Gibson-Davis, Carolyn Greenwald, Craig Higgins, Amy Howard, Ariel Kalil, Lori Kowaleski-Jones, Katherine Magnuson, Amy Meckeler, Liz Peters, Sally Stone Richmond, Jennifer Rouin, Kosali Simon, Jessica Su, Carrie Susskind, Marybeth Tarzian, and Cindy Thompson.

Spending so much time reading and writing about families gave me the opportunity to reflect on how fortunate I am to be surrounded by kind, loving, and generous family members of my own. My mother, Margaret Dunifon, always puts family first. She is a fabulous mother and a fantastic grandmother, and her love and support are unwavering and always appreciated. My father, William Dunifon, taught me to believe in myself. My sister Laura Kicklighter has brought fun and happiness to my life since before I can remember and constantly amazes me with her strength. My sister Sally Bryan shows me the meaning of love and graciousness. I gratefully remember my grandparents—Austin and Una Rudolph, Madge and Dale Dunifon—and honorary grandparents, Mamie and Lou Trubshaw. I am honored to be the aunt of nieces Maggie and Josie Kicklighter, Annie Lathrop, Mary-Kate Coughlin, and Sofia Bryan-Rago and nephews Jack Lathrop and Tommy Coughlin. I am forever grateful for the support of John Cawley Sr., Rick and Franny Roehm, Jeremy and Kathleen Coughlin, Mike Johnson, Sommer Rago, Fran and Joe Garvey, Bill Reddington, and Silke Reddington. Lastly, I remember loved family members who are no longer with us but whom I was honored to know: Cinda

Cawley, Jordan Kicklighter, John Lathrop, Dorothy Reddington, and John Reddington.

Finally, I would like to thank my husband, John Cawley, whose love, advice, and support inspired and sustained me throughout this project and with whom I am so lucky to be traveling this life. To my sons, Jimmy and Will, the love you give me is such a wonderful gift, and I am forever grateful that I get to be your mom.

Notes

Introduction

1. Calculations made using data from U.S. Census Bureau, 2014 American Community Survey. Census data can be found at https://www.census.gov/acs/www/data/data-tables-and-tools/data-profiles/2014/.

2. Barack Obama, *Dreams from My Father* (New York: Random House, 2004).

3. Donna M. Butts, *Kinship Care: Supporting Those Who Raise Our Children* (Baltimore, Md.: Annie E. Casey Foundation, 2005), http://www.aecf.org/m/resourcedoc/aecf-KinshipCareSupportingThoseRaisingOurChildren-2005.pdf.

4. Julia A. Graber and Jeanne Brooks-Gunn, "Transitions and Turning Points: Navigating the Passage from Childhood through Adolescence," *Developmental Psychology* 32, no. 4 (1996): 768–776; Lawrence. Steinberg and Jennifer S. Silk, "Parenting Adolescents," in *Handbook of Parenting*, vol. 1, 2nd ed., ed. by Marc H. Bornstein (Mahwah, N.J.: Lawrence Erlbaum Associates, 2008), 103–134.

5. Mariana Amorim, Rachel Dunifon and Natasha Pilkauskas, "The Magnitude and Timing of Grandparental Coresidence During Childhood in the United States," *Demographic Research* 37, no. 52 (2017): 1695–1706.

6. Nancy E. Reichman, Julien Teitler, Irwin Garfinkel, and Sara S. McLanahan, "Fragile Families: Sample and Design," *Children and Youth Services Review* 23, no. 4/5 (2001): 303–326.

7. Natasha Pilkauskas and Rachel Dunifon, "Understanding Grand-families: Characteristics of Grandparents, Nonresident Parents, and Children," *Journal of Marriage and Family* 78 (2016): 623–633.

8. Glen Elder, Monica Johnson, and Robert Crosnoe, "The Emergence and Development of Life Course Theory," in *Handbook of the Life Course*, ed. Jeylan Mortimer and Michael Shanahan (New York: Kluwer Academics / Plenum, 2003).

9. Martha J. Cox and Blair Paley, "Understanding Families as Systems," *Current Directions in Psychological Science* 12, no. 5 (2003): 193–196.

10. Carol B. Stack and Linda M. Burton, "Kinscripts," *Journal of Comparative Family Studies* 24, no. 2 (1993): 157–170.

11. Bruce. J. Biddle, "Recent Development in Role Theory," *Annual Review of Sociology* 12 (1986): 67–92.

12. Jan Backhouse and Anne Graham, "Grandparents Raising Grandchildren: Negotiating the Complexities of Role-Identity Conflict," *Child and Family Social Work* 17 (2011): 306–315; Deborah Langosh, "Grandparents Parenting Again: Challenges, Strengths, and Implications for Practice," *Psychoanalytic Inquiry* 32 (2012): 163–170.

13. Gregory C. Smith, Patrick A. Palmieri, Gregory R. Hancock, and Rhonda R. Richardson, "Custodial Grandmothers' Psychological Distress, Dysfunctional Parenting, and Grandchildren's Adjustment," *International Journal of Aging and Human Development* 67, no. 4 (2008): 327–357; Laura Landry-Meyer and Barbara M. Newman, "An Exploration of the Grandparental Caregiver Role," *Journal of Family Issues* 25, no. 8 (2004): 1005–1025.

14. Sara S. McLanahan, "Diverging Destinies: How Children Are Faring under the Second Demographic Transition," *Demography* 41, no. 4 (2004): 607–627; Andrew J. Cherlin, *The Marriage Go Round* (New York: Vintage, 2009); Gretchen Livingston, "Less Than Half of U.S. Kids Today Live in a 'Traditional' Family," Pew Research Center, December 22, 2014, http://www.pewresearch .org/fact-tank/2014/12/22/less-than-half-of-u-s-kids-today-live

-in-a-traditional-family/; Jane Waldfogel, Terry-Ann Craigie, and Jeanne Brooks-Gunn, "Fragile Families and Child Wellbeing," *Future of Children* 20, no. 2 (2010): 87–112, http://www.princeton .edu/futureofchildren/publications/docs/20_02_05.pdf.

15. Marcia J. Carlson and Frank F. Furstenberg, "The Prevalence and Correlates of Multipartnered Fertility among Urban U.S. Parents," *Journal of Marriage and Family* 68, no. 3 (2006): 718–732.

16. Livingston, "Fewer Than Half of U.S. Kids Today."

17. Sara McLanahan, Ron Haskins, Irwin Garfinkel, Ronald B. Mincy, and Elisabeth Donahue, "Strengthening Fragile Families," Future of Children, Policy Brief, Fall 2010, http://www .futureofchildren.org/sites/futureofchildren/files/media/fragile _families_20_02_policybrief.pdf.

18. McLanahan, "Diverging Destinies."

19. James P. Gleeson, Julia M. Wesley, Raquel Ellis, Claire Seryak, Glen Walls Talley, and Jackie Robinson, "Becoming Involved in Raising a Relative's Child: Reasons, Caregiver Motivations, and Pathways to Informal Kinship Care," *Child and Family Social Work* 14, no. 3 (2009): 300–310; Margaret Platt Jendrick, "Grandparents Who Parent Their Grandchildren: Circumstances and Decisions," *Gerontologist* 34 (1994): 206–216.

20. Butts, *Kinship Care.*

21. Langosh, "Grandparents Parenting Again."

22. Heather J. Bachman and P. Lindsay Chase-Lansdale, "Custodial Grandmothers' Physical, Mental, and Economic Well-Being: Comparisons of Primary Caregivers from Low-Income Neighborhoods," *Family Relations* 54, no. 4 (2005): 475–487; Carol M. Musil and Muayyad Ahmad, "The Health of Grandmothers: A Comparison by Caregiver Status," *Journal of Aging and Health* 14, no. 1 (2002): 96–121; Laura D. Pittman, "Grandmothers' Involvement among Young Adolescents Growing Up in Poverty," *Journal of Research on Adolescence* 17, no. 1 (2007): 89–116; Susan J. Kelly, Deborah M. Whitley, and Peter E. Campos, "African American Caregiving Grandmothers: Results of an

Intervention to Improve Health Indicators and Health Promotion Behaviors," *Journal of Family Nursing* 19, no. 1 (2012): 53–73; Gregory C. Smith and Patrick A. Palmieri, "Risk of Psychological Difficulties among Children Raised by Custodial Grandparents," *Psychiatric Services* 58, no. 10 (2007): 1303–1310; Catherine Chase Goodman and Merril Silverstein, "Grandmothers Raising Grandchildren: Ethnic and Racial Differences in Well-Being among Custodial and Coparenting Families," *Journal of Family Issues* 27, no. 11 (2006): 1605–1626; Bert Hayslip and Patricia L. Kaminski, "Grandparents Raising Their Grandchildren," *Marriage and Family Review* 37, no. 1/2 (2005): 147–169; Lynne M. Casper and Kenneth R. Bryson, "Coresident Grandparents and Their Grandchildren: Grandparent Maintained Families" (presentation, Annual Meeting of the Population Association of America, Chicago, Ill., May 1998), https://www.census.gov/population/www/documentation/twps0026/twps0026.html.

23. Meredith Minkler and Esme Fuller-Thomson, "The Health of Grandparents Raising Grandchildren: Results of a National Study," *American Journal of Public Health* 89, no. 9 (1999): 1384–1389.

24. Megan L. Dolbin-MacNab and Margaret K. Keiley, "Navigating Interdependence: How Adolescents Raised Solely by Grandparents Experience Their Family Relationships," *Family Relations* 58, no. 2 (2009): 162–175; Catherin Chase Goodman and Merril Silverstein, "Grandmothers Who Parent Their Grandchildren: An Exploratory Study of Close Relations across Three Generations," *Journal of Family Issues* 22, no. 5 (2001): 557–578.

25. Yolanda R. Green and Catherine Chase Goodman, "Understanding Birth Parent Involvement in Kinship Families: Influencing Factors and the Importance of Placement Arrangement," *Children and Youth Services Review* 32 (2010): 1357–1364; Goodman and Silverstein, "Grandmothers Who Parent Their Grandchildren"; Smith et al., "Custodial Grandmothers' Psychological Distress."

26. Langosh, "Grandparents Parenting Again."

27. Jill Theresa Messing, "From the Child's Perspective: A Qualitative Analysis of Kinship Care Placements," *Children and Youth Services Review* 28, no. 12 (2006): 1415–1434; Dolbin-MacNab and Keiley, "Navigating Interdependence."

28. Megan L. Dolbin-MacNab, "Just Like Raising Your Own? Grandmothers' Perceptions of Parenting a Second Time Around," *Family Relations* 55, no. 5 (2006): 564–575.

29. Langosh, "Grandparents Parenting Again."

30. Melissa M. Dolan, Celia Casanueva, Keith R. Smith, and Robert H. Bradley, "Parenting and the Home Environment Provided by Grandmothers of Children in the Child Welfare System," *Children and Youth Services Review* 21 (2009): 784–796.

31. Dolbin-MacNab and Keiley, "Navigating Interdependence."

32. Dolbin-MacNab and Keiley, "Navigating Interdependence"; Dolbin-MacNab, "Just Like Raising Your Own?"

1. What Leads to the Formation of Grandfamilies?

1. Natasha Pilkauskas and Rachel Dunifon, "Understanding Grandfamilies: Characteristics of Grandparents, Nonresident Parents, and Children," *Journal of Marriage and Family* 78 (2016): 623–633.

2. Barbara H. Fiese and Arnold J. Sameroff, "The Family Narrative Consortium: A Multidimensional Approach to Narratives," *Monographs of the Society for Research in Child Development* 64, no. 2 (1999): 1–36; Dan P. McAdams, "The Psychology of Life Stories," *Review of General Psychology* 5, no. 2 (2001): 100–122.

2. "I Couldn't Be Prouder to Be the Caregiver of You"

1. Andrew J. Cherlin, "Remarriage as an Incomplete Institution," *American Journal of Sociology* 84, no. 3 (1978): 634–650; Andrew J. Cherlin and Frank F. Furstenberg, "Stepfamilies in the United States: A Reconsideration," *Annual Review of Sociology* 20 (1994): 359–381.

2. Cherlin, "Remarriage."

3. Gunhild O. Hagestad and Linda M. Burton, "Grandparenthood, Life Context, and Family Development," *American Behavioral Scientist* 29, no. 4 (1986): 471.

4. Gunhild. O. Hagestad and Bernice L. Neugarten, "Age and the Life Course," in *Handbook of Aging and the Social Sciences*, ed. Robert H. Binstock and Ethel Shanas (New York: Van Nostrand Reinhold, 1985), 2, 35–61.

5. Linda M. Burton, Peggye Dilworth-Anderson, and Cynthia Merriweather-deVries, "Context and Surrogate Parenting among Contemporary Grandparents," *Marriage and Family Review* 20 (2010): 349–366.

6. Andrea G. Hunter and Robert J. Taylor, "Grandparenthood in African American Families," in *Handbook on Grandparenthood*, ed. Maximiliane Szinovacz (Westport, Conn.: Greenwood Press, 1998), 70–86.

7. Linda M. Burton and Cynthia Devries, "Challenges and Rewards: African American Grandparents as Surrogate Parents," *Generations* 16, no. 3 (1992): 51–55.

3. "I Get All the Love I Need"

1. James E. Cote and Charles Levine, "A Formulation of Erikson's Theory of Ego Identity Formation," *Developmental Review* 7 (1987): 273–325; Laurence Steinberg, "We Know Some Things: Parent–Adolescent Relationships in Retrospect and Prospect," *Journal of Research on Adolescence* 11, no. 1 (2001): 1–19; Harold D. Grotevant, "Toward a Process Model of Identity Formation," *Journal of Adolescent Research* 2, no. 3 (1987): 203–222.

2. Mary Louis Arnold, Michael W. Pratt, and Cheryl Hicks, "Adolescents' Representations of Parents' Voices in Family Stories: Value Lessons, Personal Adjustment, and Identity Development," in *Family Stories and the Life Course*, ed. Michael W. Pratt and Barbara H. Fiese (Mahwah, N.J.: Lawrence Erlbaum, 2004), 163–186.

3. Dan P. McAdams, "The Psychology of Life Stories," *Review of General Psychology* 5, no. 2 (2001): 101.

4. Steinberg, "We Know Some Things."

5. Grotevant, "Toward a Process Model," 215.

6. Robyn Fivush, Jennifer Bohanek, Rachel Robertson, and Marshall Duke, "Family Narratives and the Development of Children's Emotional Well-Being," in *Family Stories and the Life Course*, ed. Michael W. Pratt and Barbara H. Fiese (Mahwah, N.J.: Lawrence Erlbaum, 2004), 55–76.

7. Sabrina Koepke and Jaap J. A. Denissen, "Dynamics of Identity Development and Separation–Individuation in Parent–Child Relationships during Adolescence and Emerging Adulthood—a Conceptual Integration," *Developmental Review* 32, no. 1 (2012): 67–88.

8. Nora Dunbar and Harold D. Grotevant, "Adoption Narratives: The Construction of Adoptive History during Adolescence," in *Family Stories and the Life Course*, ed. Michael W. Pratt and Barbara H. Fiese (Mahwah, N.J.: Lawrence Erlbaum, 2004), 135–162.

9. Harold D. Grotevant, Nora Dunbar, Julie K. Kohler, and Amy M. Lash Esau, "Adoptive Identity: How Contexts within and beyond the Family Shape Developmental Pathways," *Family Relations* 49, no. 4 (2000): 379–387.

10. Julie K. Kohler, Harold D. Grotevant, and Ruth G. McRoy, "Adopted Adolescents' Preoccupation with Adoption: The Impact on Adoptive Family Relationships," *Journal of Marriage and Family* 64 (2002): 93–104.

4. "I Love My Daughter, but I Don't Like Her Right about Now"

1. Natasha Pilkauskas and Rachel Dunifon, "Understanding Grandfamilies: Characteristics of Grandparents, Nonresident Parents, and Children," *Journal of Marriage and Family* 78 (2016): 623–633.

2. Rachel Dunifon, Kimberly Kopko, P. Lindsay Chase-Lansdale, and Lauren Wakschlag, "Multigenerational Relationships in

Families with Custodial Grandparents," in *Grandparenting in the U.S.*, ed. Madonna Harrington Meyer and Ynesse Adbul-Malak (New York: Baywood, 2016): 133–160.

3. Carol B. Stack and Linda M. Burton, "Kinscripts," *Journal of Comparative Family Studies* 24, no. 2 (1993): 157–170; Martha J. Cox and Blair Paley, "Understanding Families as Systems," *Current Directions in Psychological Science* 12 (2003): 193–196.

4. James McHale, Inna Khazan, Pauline Erera, Tamir Rotman, Wendy DeCourcey, and Melanie McConnell, "Coparenting in Diverse Family Systems," in *Handbook of Parenting*, vol. 3, 2nd ed., ed. Marc H. Bornstein (Mahwah, N.J.: Lawrence Erlbaum Associates, 2008), 75–108; Joan B. Kelly and Robert E. Emery, "Children's Adjustment Following Divorce: Risk and Resilience Perspectives," *Family Relations* 52, no. 4 (2003): 352–362.

5. Policies and Programs to Address Grandfamilies' Needs

1. Rebecca McBride, *Having a Voice and a Choice: New York State Handbook for Relatives Raising Children* (Albany: New York State Office of Children and Family Services and New York State Office of Temporary and Disability Assistance, 2010), http://ocfs .ny.gov/main/publications/Pub5080.pdf.

2. "Children in Kinship Care," Urban Institute, 2002, accessed October 2017, http://www.urban.org/sites/default/files/publication/ 59751/900661-Children-in-Kinship-Care.PDF.

3. "Title IV-E Guardianship Assistance," Children's Bureau, U.S. Department of Health and Human Services, July 26, 2013, http:// www.acf.hhs.gov/cb/resource/title-iv-e-guardianship-assistance.

4. Child Welfare Information Gateway, *Major Federal Legislation Concerned with Child Protection, Child Welfare, and Adoption* (Washington, D.C.: U.S. Department of Health and Human Services, Children's Bureau, 2016), https://www.childwelfare.gov/ pubpdfs/majorfedlegis.pdf.

5. Elizabeth A. Courtney-Long, Dianna D. Carroll, Qing C. Zhang, Alissa C. Stevens, Shannon Griffin-Blake, Brian S. Armour, and Vincent A. Campbell, "Key Findings: Prevalence of Disability and Disability Type among Adults—United States, 2013," Centers for Disease Control and Prevention, *Morbidity and Mortality Weekly Report*, July 31, 2015, https://www.cdc.gov/mmwr/preview/mmwrhtml/mm6429a2.htm?s_cid=mm6429a2_w.

6. Natasha Pilkauskas and Rachel Dunifon, "Understanding Grand-families: Characteristics of Grandparents, Nonresident Parents, and Children," *Journal of Marriage and Family* 78 (2016): 623–633.

7. Carol M. Musil and Ahmad Muayyad, "The Health of Grand-mothers: A Comparison by Caregiver Status," *Journal of Aging and Health* 14, no. 1 (2002): 96–121; Bert Hayslip Jr. and Patricia L. Kaminski, "Grandparents Raising Their Grandchildren: A Review of the Literature and Suggestions for Practice," *Gerontologist* 45, no. 2 (2005): 262–269.

8. "Eligibility and Cost," New York State Department of Health, accessed October 2017, https://www.health.ny.gov/health_care/child_health_plus/eligibility_and_cost.htm.

9. Natasha Pilkauskas and Rachel Dunifon, "Children Living with Grandparents: Prevalence, Characteristics and Complexity" (unpublished manuscript, 2016).

10. "Project Healthy Grandparents," Georgia State University, accessed December 2017, http://phg.snhp.gsu.edu/.

11. Susan J. Kelley, Beatrice Crofts Yorker, Deborah M. Whitley, and Theresa A. Sipe, "A Multimodal Intervention for Grandparents Raising Grandchildren: Results of an Exploratory Study," *Child Welfare* 80, no. 1 (2001): 27–50; Susan J. Kelley, Deborah M. Whit-ley, and Peter E. Campos, "Grandmothers Raising Grandchildren: Results of an Intervention to Improve Health Outcomes," *Journal of Nursing Scholarship* 42, no. 4 (2010): 379–386.

12. Anne Strozier, LaSandra McGrew, Kerry Krishman, and Aaaron Smith, "Kinship Care Connection: A School-Based Intervention

for Kinship Caregivers and the Children in Their Care," *Children and Youth Services Review* 27 (2005): 1011–1029.

13. "2011–2015 American Community Survey 5-Year Estimates," U.S. Census Bureau, American Fact Finder, accessed December 2017, https://factfinder.census.gov/faces/tableservices/jsf/pages/productview.xhtml?pid=ACS_15_5YR_DP03&src=pt.

14. Jane Mauldon, Richard Speiglman, Christina Sogar, and Matt Stagner, "TANF Child-Only Cases: Who Are They? What Policies Affect Them? What Is Being Done?," December 11, 2012.

15. Mauldon et al., "TANF Child-Only Cases."

16. Pilkauskas and Dunifon, "Children Living with Grandparents."

17. Kimberly Kopko, "Parenting Styles and Adolescents," Cornell University Cooperative Extension, 2007, https://www.human.cornell.edu/sites/default/files/PAM/Parenting/Parenting-20Styles-20and-20Adolescents.pdf.

18. Rachel E. Dunifon and Emi DiSciullo, "Kinship Care and Communication: Family Portraits Project Helping Teens Tell Their Stories," accessed September 2017 https://www.human.cornell.edu/sites/default/files/PAM/Parenting/Kinship-care-and-communication-1.pdf.

19. Kopko, "Parenting Styles and Adolescents."

20. "Parenting a Second Time Around (PASTA)," Cornell University, College of Human Ecology, accessed September 2017, http://www.human.cornell.edu/pam/outreach/parenting/academic/parentingasecondtimearound.cfm. PASTA curriculum created by Jennifer Birkmayer, Isabelle Jensen, Denyse Variano, and Gerard Wallace.

21. Eliza Lathrop Cook and Kimberly Kopko, "Outcomes of Participants in the Cornell Cooperative Extension Parenting a Second Time Around Program," 2014, https://www.human.cornell.edu/sites/default/files/PAM/Parenting/PASTA/PASTA_Orange-County-2014-Report_Final-2.pdf.

Appendix

1. Lauren S. Wakschlag, P. Lindsay Chase-Lansdale, and Jeanne Brooks-Gunn, "Not Just 'Ghosts in the Nursery': Contemporaneous Intergenerational Relationships and Parenting in Youth African-American Families," *Child Development* 67, no. 5 (1996): 2131–2147.

2. Janet M. Melby, Rand D. Conger, R. Book, M. Rueter, L. Lucy, D. Repinski, S. Rogers, B. Rogers, and L. Scaramella, *The Iowa Family Interaction Rating Scales*, 5th ed. (Ames, Iowa: Institute for Social and Behavioral Research, Iowa State University, 1998).

Index

Page numbers followed by *t* refer to tables.

About the Author

RACHEL E. DUNIFON is a professor in the Department of Policy Analysis and Management and senior associate dean in the College of Human Ecology at Cornell University. She received a BA from Davidson College and a PhD from Northwestern University. Dunifon's research is in the area of child and family policy, with a focus on factors influencing the development of less-advantaged children. In her spare time, she enjoys spending time with her husband, children, and friends; reading; running; and yoga.

Available titles in the Rutgers Series in Childhood Studies: